CARRIED BY THE CURRENT

Carried by the Current
A Benedictine Perspective

Ambrose Tinsley OSB

the columba press

First published in 2004 by
the columba press
55A Spruce Avenue, Stillorgan Industrial Park,
Blackrock, Co Dublin

Cover by Liam Furlong
Origination by The Columba Press
Illustrations by Máire Kennedy
Printed in Ireland by ColourBooks Ltd, Dublin

ISBN 1 85607 458 7

Copyright © 2004, Ambrose Tinsley OSB

Table of Contents

Preface	9
Introduction	11

PART ONE

Lectio
The Power of the Creative word … 17
Exploration of the Scriptures:
    Entering the River … 21
    The Tapestry … 26
    The View from the Top … 31

Prayer
Four essays:
    Awareness … 36
    Loving Words … 42
    An Underlying Quality … 47
    Trinitarian Reality … 52
The Spirit & the Bride … 57

Work
Work, a Benedictine Insight … 58

PART TWO

Who do you say that I am? … 69
Christ, the Inclusive Person … 73
Do We Need a Trinity? … 78
Is God a Father or a Mother – or just Nothing? … 83
'The Love of God' – What does that mean? … 89
Spirit of Life … 94

PART THREE

Hospitality	101
The Building of Community:	
Far & Near	106
Becoming Middle People	111
The Jig-Saw Puzzle	116
A Dream Unfolds	117
Appendix	
We Dare to Say 'Our Father'	121
References	127

List of Illustrations

Page 8: 'The Man of God, Benedict.'
Page 16: Stool-symbol of Benedict's three-fold plan for life
Page 68: The Inviting Trinity
Page 100: 'Little Pieces'
Page 120: The Opening Words of the Lord's Prayer

Preface

This book began with some short essays which included three on how to think about the scriptures as we read them for ourselves. However, all were the result of conversations which I had with different people, either here at my own monastery or when lecturing in another place. They consequently echo many thoughts which I myself received, even if the final synthesis is mine.

My starting point, it should be noted, is not that of individuals who seek their personal fulfilment. It is that of the inspiring life which they themselves receive from people who have gone before them and from many others who in different ways impinge upon their daily lives. Indeed, it is the life which ultimately comes from God and which, through those who are our fellow-pilgrims, can then help us on our often struggling way to him.

There is an all-embracing breadth in this. It is that of the Spirit which ennobles ours and which can lead us to perceive and to accept the caring and creative Word which comes in many different ways. Then, as that Word becomes alive in each of us, each one of us can grow into what each of us is called to be. We, thereby, are united to the One in whom that Word was incarnated in a very special way and so, through him, enabled to desire with confidence the Promised Land of Life Unlimited which everyone desires.

In trying to explain in feeble words this Trinitarian dimension to our lives, I am indebted to all those who have in different ways assisted me in the writing of this book. Among those I am very grateful to Fr Eugene Duffy who agreed to read it at a fairly early stage and then to make a number of encouraging remarks. I also want to thank Fr Tom Jordan OP for his reading of the nearly finished text and for the pertinent suggestions which he made. Then a special 'thank you' goes to Sr Phyllis Moynihan for her many contributions which were valuable and even necessary as successive chapters were considered and composed. Moreover, as our words can often be inadequate and certainly can be supported by the visual arts, our thanks are also due to Máire Kennedy for offering the illustrations which begin each section of this book. I finally need to thank my own community for helping me to recognise, and over many years to make my own, the truths which for the reader are presented here.

Introduction

Life is at times unbalanced.
This is true, particularly in our modern and western world. The pressures to be doing this or that or something else are very great and even tend to multiply. No doubt for many people such activity can be both satisfying and at times exciting and that frequently is good. But is there not a part of all of us which sooner or later seems to scream: 'but what of me?' 'Do I not also need to be considered and fulfilled?' Yet, even while that is the case, there are a lot of people who are so caught up in the unending and demanding treadmill of their lives that they are barely conscious of their inner voice. Indeed the fact that some of them may hear it does not mean that they will always cope with what it seems to say or that they will not think that there is nothing they can do at all. But those who do respond and consequently change their way of living often find, not just a better balance in their lives, but also an ability to give much more to people whom they meet than just some kind of relatively superficial help.
Today there are a lot of books available which can help those who want to understand a little more about their frequently neglected needs and many of them will suggest how they should be addressed. However, let me introduce the way of one who guided many people down the ages to a lifestyle in which they could truly grow. His name was Benedict.[1] He came from Nursia, a town in Italy, and after many years became the author of a famous 'Rule for Monks'[2] which, by its openness and wisdom, has become a valuable guide for many non-monastics too. Although he did not use the 'balance' word, he consequently did provide for those who were to follow him a way of life in which three fundamental needs which everybody has can be progressively fulfilled. Thus anyone who really listens to him comes to understand that work is not to dominate their lives yet, on the other hand, that it should be considered as intrinsic to their spiritual growth and so, as much as possible, be well-chosen and well-done. Moreover, when they find that with some effort work will stay within its proper boundaries, they may also find that they have time for prayer, both in the company of others

and alone. Indeed some Benedictine houses of the nineteenth century liked to paint the motto 'prayer and work' (in Latin: *ora et labora*) on their walls and such a motto can be useful still. But if we find we are attracted to it, we should note that Benedict was also conscious of a third important need, one which concerned the mind. He therefore allocated quite a lot of time for *lectio*, that is for quietly absorbing both the words and insights of the spiritual authors of the past.

There surely is a message for us here.

However, since our lives today can be so different from those for whom the Rule of Benedict was written there would seem to be some problems too. For instance, work for many people in this present age is much less manual than it was for his original disciples. Therefore, it is often not the kind which will allow the mind to rest and silently digest the thoughts which had in some way been acquired. Instead a lot of work today is likely to absorb, not just more time than was the case before, but also much more energy as well. The consequence is, not just that the worker lacks the mentally-relaxing time which manual work can often offer but that he or she is forced to look for relaxation in non-mental ways. Thus the demands of *lectio* can also be ignored and so a second element of Benedictine balance may not even have a chance to be accepted as a necessary part of life. As for the element of prayer, the pressures of society, which have already changed the nature of much work and so of reading-possibilities, can also have on it a limiting effect, if they do not exclude it altogether from the menu of our lives. So our initial task is to consider if and how the three-pronged formula which Benedict accepted for the daily life of his communities can be today of any use at all.

Let us begin at least by recognising that these items, work and prayer and *lectio*, are all connected with the fundamental needs of body, mind and spirit. They, consequently, are important, so they must in some way be addressed. But how? To answer that I could suggest that we begin by treasuring any moments in our daily or our weekly lives when we can be engaged in manual activity and at the same time let our minds relax. Then certainly at other times we should do all we can to stock those minds of ours with useful thoughts so that, as people can relax within a room well-furnished, we will find that is it possible to stop and be at peace within ourselves. That does not necessarily mean that we must spend a lot of time at *lectio* itself but that we probably will come to realise that it should be included as a valuable part of our own mental fare. And finally concerning prayer: we should, I would suggest, review our lives and then identify those times which we could put aside in order to allow our minds to concentrate on God's all-loving presence and, if possible, to be still. Then, even though society today is different from what it was in Benedict's time, we may discover that we have at least improved the balance in our lives.

However, having mentioned these three needs which Benedict acknowledged, we could note that it is frequently the mental one which has to be considered and protected most. It is the hinge between the other two. As one wise writer, whom I can no longer name, once wrote: 'if the mind is nourished well the body is more likely to relax and then to do what it is told while one's own spirit is in consequence more likely to be free'. So choosing what we want to think about and also how to think about it is of very great importance. That does not mean that there are some things which must never be allowed into our minds. That certainly would be exaggerated censorship. But it suggests that if whatever is being thought about is not perceived in its relationship to everything, including God, it will not ever be correctly understood. Indeed it may appear in a distorted form and then of course it may distort the thinker too. But, on the other hand, a mind which is both disciplined and cultivated through some form of *lectio* will find it easier to discern what should be done while it will also offer us material which can facilitate our prayer.

This brings us to the second section of this book.

While the former section focused on some fundamental needs which no one can afford to overlook, this second part concerns the people who are part of our own lives. It recognises that through their own words and deeds God can and does reveal himself and will continue doing so. That is of course what happens when the words of someone who had been inspired are read and pondered in the heart. But it is also what can happen through the people whom we meet each day and no doubt in a special way through some. Indeed it is what happens in an extra special way for many people when they think about or enter into a relationship with Jesus whom they recognise as one in whom the fullness of divinity abides.

But let us note that in such cases there is always the activity of 'someone' else. It is that of the unseen Spirit which can work in those who offer us some guidance or some help and then which can dispose us to perceive and to accept the blessing which is thereby being offered. Certainly the work of that disposing Spirit can be hindered by a lack of sensitivity in either party but because that Spirit comes from the creative Father it is likely that it will eventually succeed in all it does. Our task, however, in the meanwhile is to recognise the presence of that Spirit and to let it teach us how to listen to whoever comes and then, while treating them with due respect, to make our own the blessing which the all-wise Father wants to offer us through them. Then hopefully that Spirit will express through us a greater sense of peaceful gratitude and, at the same time, help us to perceive how we, in turn, can help those whom we meet.

The last and third part of this book concerns the element of personal and social growth.

If the initial chapter is entitled 'hospitality', what it implies is what I have already indicated, that is that we let the Spirit work within us so that we are able to respect and then to welcome all who come, no matter who or what they are. Then while they may be helped in some way by the welcome they receive, we certainly will grow through our own openness to them and, as the sons and daughters of the all-embracing God, to him from whom such people ultimately come. The second chapter moves on to consider how God uses our relationships with one another to create the true community that he desires. This leads us to the final chapter which looks forward to what is to come. We may, of course, not always think about that final goal and sometimes we may even doubt that it is there at all. However there is always part of us which will at certain times remind us that it has to be. Indeed, if God has poured his Spirit into ours, he certainly will satisfy our deepest yearning which is for a life which is, not only perfect in itself, but also without end.

So once again we sense the trinitarian design which is in everything and which is certainly the major underlying theme in all the chapters of this book.

It is unfortunate that this design has been so undervalued in the western church as circumstances and its innate attitude to life developed in more manageable and often legalistic ways. However, the more spiritual understanding was not ever fully lost. It could and often did find its expression in the simple words and private prayers of ordinary people and perhaps there is a residue of that when someone speaks about the 'spirit of' whatever must be done. In any case there is in recent years a new appreciation, not just of the self, but also of the Spirit which can guide us in all that we do. This is a very welcome counter-balance to what can so easily become a hierarchical and over legalistic attitude but it is not enough. There is another need. It is to let that Spirit which we can receive help us to recognise a totally transcendent Source for everything. We may refer to such a Source as 'Father', and we should, but in the end we know that something in us needs a Being which is far beyond all names and, therefore, so unlimited that we, and everybody, have a chance to grow. So in the end we need three 'things'. We need a 'body', personal and social, which can organise itself to the advantage of its many parts; we need a Spirit which can animate each individual and the social 'body' as a whole, and finally we need to recognise a totally transcendent Presence which is both the source of all that happens and the goal of everything as well. In other words we need a Trinity. It is the only way that all things can be one.

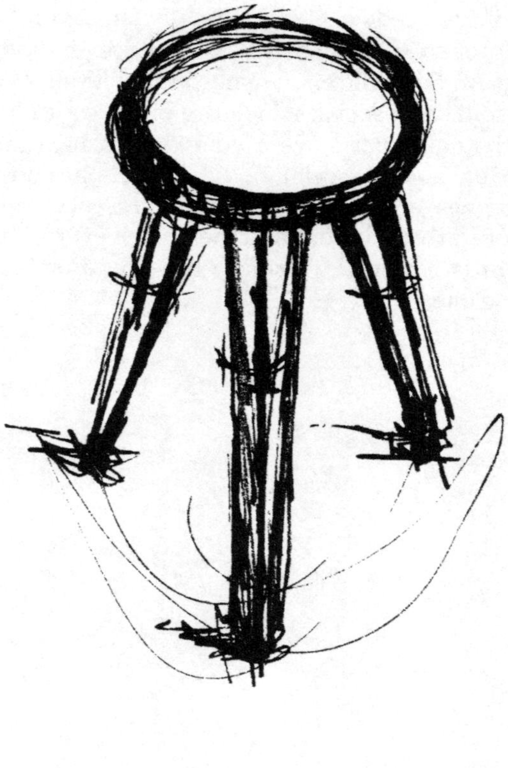

PART ONE

Lectio

As the rain and the snow come down from heaven
and return not thither but water the earth,
making it bring forth and sprout,
giving seed to the sower and bread to the eater,
so shall my word be.
It goes forth from my mouth
and shall not return to me empty
but shall accomplish all that I purpose
and prosper in the thing
for which I sent it. *(Isaiah 55:10-11)*

The Power of the Creative Word

'Take and Read. Take and Read.' These are the words which so impressed the young Augustine[1] that he went to where his Bible was and, having opened it at random, read the words which then immediately caught his eye. That moment was to be for him a very special one and later on, when looking back on his own life, he saw it as a most important milestone in his quest. It was. However, let us note that when he was describing that event he was aware that there were other people who in ways which were quite similar had also come to recognise what they should do. He mentioned in particular a famous desert monk called Anthony[2] who, on entering a nearby church, had been so struck by what the gospel passage which was being read proclaimed that he obeyed it and, by doing so in his particular way, became for many others after him a model to be followed. So we have examples from the lives of two important people to encourage us in turn 'to take and read', or simply hear, the scriptures and to let the given word both touch and influence the way we live each day.

What I am saying here is not meant to imply that every time

we take our Bibles and at random read some passage we will find exciting verses which will suddenly transform our lives. That would be too much to expect. But on the other hand it certainly is true that each and every verse of scripture did contain a vital meaning for those people who first heard it and that was of course the very reason why it was remembered and preserved. Our problem, therefore, often is that when we hear or read some words of scripture we may just presume that we have not been in a comparable situation and that consequently they are just irrelevant to us. It, therefore, would not be a bad idea to do some formal study, either by ourselves or in the context of some group. However, since a lot of people may not have the time or energy or even opportunity for that, it might be good to look at certain simple ways whereby we can at least discern which sections of the Bible are important for us and which should from time to time be read.

Let me begin by mentioning a very simple rule of thumb. It is that, when we open our own Bibles, we should note than any passage which we read is only one of three quite different types. The first are those which can console us and of course we tend to like them and, perhaps, to mark them so that we can find them quickly when we want to savour their refreshing words again. They are the passages which tell us where, or who, we are. The second kind are those which offer us a challenge if we read them with an open heart and mind. They are the passages which tell us where we ought to be. As for the third kind, they are all the other ones which for the moment seem to have no relevance for us at all. So, even though they might be very useful for us in the future, for the moment we can simply tell ourselves that they are for another day. Then we can focus on the ones which seem to help us most.

To go a little deeper one could follow some suggested list of passages which can be used for different and particular occasions and at times that can be quite a useful method. But the one which has an extra value is to read the sections which are allocated in the lectionary for the liturgy (or Mass) of every day. This method will bring those who use it through a number of the books of scripture every year, although a three-year cycle is in place as well.[3] It consequently can provide a relatively gentle yet effective introduction to the Bible as a whole. Of course this will not guarantee that every passage which is read will always answer some immediate or urgent need. Indeed a friend of mine who had been following this method for a while admitted that at times the words she read did not mean anything to her at all. They were presumably among those which were 'for another day'. However she could also write that there were other times when what she read was so significant that she would store it in her memory for future pondering. The words she read, she said, spoke of a God who loved her and who would not ever let her down. We too, as we plough through the lectionary, can quite often come across such life-infusing words and when we do should we not also happily absorb the message they contain?

However, let us note that this same method can present us with a challenge too. It can remind us that the word is spoken, not just to each person as an individual, but also to a whole community just as it was when it was uttered first. So when we come to read a passage of the scriptures it implicitly invites us to consider that it often is through other people that we can receive what has been promised through the words which we have read. Then, however, we may also come to realise that others may not benefit from what that passage indicates unless it comes to them through us! So God who loves and cares for all his people wills to work through each of them so that all will receive what he desires to give.

But as we reach out to our fellow-Christians and to others we may come to recognise another truth. It is that the inspiring Word which comes from God is also an enabling one. To put that in a negative, yet very telling, way let me here introduce a woman of Nigeria who used to start her day by praying with some others in their parish church. Then, when on one occasion she was working in the nearby open market, she espied the local catechist who had been passing by. She beckoned him and said: 'A little while ago I was about to do what I knew I should not do, but I thought of what you read and said this morning and I didn't.' There the word of God which had been heard and obviously pondered bore its own fruit in a good and conscientious person's life, and no doubt she had many times fulfilled its positive requirements too.

This is perhaps the moment to consider that the word that comes from God, however strong, will not be fruitful in our lives if we are not disposed to welcome it. For that the Spirit has a part to play. Did not St Paul when writing to the church at Corinth indicate that this is so when he declared that no one knows the mind of God unless that person is assisted by the Spirit that comes to us from above?[4] So every time we read or listen to the Word, we will require the Spirit to enable us to understand the meaning it contains. Then, as that word becomes alive in us, that same disposing Spirit will be working once again. It will be helping us to do what it implies so that, not only we, but many others too will be affected by it and enriched.

The opening chapter of the Bible seems to indicate this same inspiring truth. It says, poetically, that the Spirit came and hovered over all the 'tohubohu', or confusion, which existed and that it was only when that had occurred that God's own word was able to make all things what they were supposed to be. It certainly is not too difficult to see how relevant that message is to our own lives today. In plainer words, the Spirit must come down on us and it must calm our frequently distracted minds. Then, when we have received the word which comes from God we will not only grow into his image and his likeness, but also be enabled to communicate it in some way to all those whom we meet and who themselves have been disposed to welcome it.

However, that creative word will probably not work as quickly in own lives as those verses of the Book of Genesis suggest. So, after we have read some passage in the scriptures and have thought about it for a while, it is important not to close the book until we have identified a verse which we can take away to ponder later on. In that way it itself will find new opportunities to worm its way into our lives as we, from different situations, come to see what it implies. This is a thought that was suggested by an under-quoted sentence of Columba Marmion, the Irish priest who joined the Benedictine Monastery of Maredsous in Belgium and became its Abbot and a Spiritual Guide to many of his time and century. When writing to a correspondent in the nineteen-twenties, he declared: 'the principal source of prayer is to be found in Holy Scripture, read with devotion and reverence and laid up in the heart'.[5] Those words deserve to be remembered and, perhaps, inscribed in our own copy of the Bible. Then the word of God will have a better opportunity, not just to teach us how to pray, but also to reach out through all we do and say into our own so frequently confused but always life-desiring world.

Entering the River

Near where I am living now the river Shannon flows. Its long and varied course began most probably with just a spring, a trickle and some pools which overflowed. I never had the opportunity to visit that initial spot but soon those waters must have turned into a stream which gradually grew as other streams became its tributaries. Then, as it continued on and gathered to itself the waters of the countryside, it finally became the mighty river which I know and which continues on until it meets the all-embracing sea.

This image of a flowing river is, as I have found, a good one to describe the value of converging with the scriptures every day.

So let us start by thinking of ourselves as small and yet enthusiastic tributaries. Then, when we take up the scriptures and begin to read, we will not only meet the sacred text, but also enter a tradition which already has been flowing down through many, many centuries. So, as we ponder what the passage which we have been reading says, we may be frequently, and even without knowing it, absorbing with it thoughts which come from people who had pondered that same passage and who then had shared with their contemporaries what it had meant for them. That is how a tradition grows. So, when in our own turn we let ourselves be influenced by all that that tradition brings, it may be worthwhile noting that, like every other tributary, we may make our own particular contribution to the mighty river as it journeys on to generations yet to come.

Before reflecting any more upon our merging with the sacred scripture, may I use this metaphor to illustrate the wider and more fundamental flow of human history. To do this let each one of us consider his or her own life, how it began and how it is forever yearning for fulfilment and indeed for the transcendence of itself.

It bubbled up
and rippled over stones,
then wandered through uncertain ways
and sometimes even seemed to change its course
although it will, we know, continue moving on

until it reaches its predestined goal
which is the great unending sea.

At times it may have met
some other streams;
or flowed into a river
which enriched it
and it still may flow into a greater one
before it reaches that absorbing ocean
which it has not ever ceased to seek.

The wonder is
that none of this would ever happen
if the infant stream
had not itself been formed and nourished
by the waters of that far off ocean
which then seems
to draw it to itself.

In this we have an image of the movement and direction of our human lives. It, therefore, can keep on reminding us, not only of the goal for which we have been made, but also of the fact that we will meet and merge in different ways with many others as we travel on and on.

So now let us recall, if possible, the time when we began to sample something of the scriptural tradition and to find that it was to our taste. For me that probably was when I listened to the bedtime stories which my parents used to read to me. But then my gradual involvement must have grown and 'rippled over stones' when I was reading to myself (while Sunday Mass was being celebrated!) all the gospel sections which were printed in a pocket missal which I had. But why am I revealing that? It is because when people, who have reached the stage of wanting to explore the scriptures, ask me how they should begin I always have, as I have intimated, the desire to offer them a list of references to the sections which have been assigned to each day's celebration of the liturgy. That will, I know, present them with at least a manageable guide. But let us note that it can also offer them a social and perhaps inspiring thought. It is that as they are reflecting on the designated passage, they are actually being joined by many, many others who throughout the world, and maybe even at that very moment, are involved in that same, hopefully transforming exercise.

However, to return to my own journey I continued and in doing so discovered not just that the four evangelists had something interesting to say, but also that a number of the other authors could be very helpful too. That new discovery, I must admit was made, not while I was still growing up, but later when I had become a monk within a Benedictine monastery. The life which as an adult I adopted there, provided me with time to read and ponder all that had been written in the sacred books. That was itself a very precious gift and later when I realised that life was likely to become more complicated I decided that, no matter what would happen, I would still give half an hour each day to reading and to pondering the message which those different books revealed. It was a good decision for in fact it was the ever deeper understanding of that message which since then has carried me along.

Of course, not everyone will manage to afford that length of time. For many people life is much too full and even pressurised. Yet if they organise themselves they may discover, as so many have, that there are always certain possibilities each day for dipping into what the scriptures say. Then, if and when they enter into some part of that flowing river, they may find perhaps to their surprise the useful or inspiring word which at that moment they in fact require. That happens, and it will without a doubt encourage them, especially perhaps if they had felt they were travelling in 'uncertain ways'. Indeed the river which they sometimes timorously enter will keep on inviting them while making its own way towards the all-embracing sea.

The person who has found already that attention to the words of scripture has encouraged him or her may also come to realise that there are different currents in the River of Tradition and that, consequently, what is most important is to let oneself be drawn towards the central one. But how, one may enquire, is that to be discerned? My answer at the moment is that it is that which can, not only carry us towards the all-embracing goal, but also in the process make us more attractive to all others who in their own ways are struggling in the same direction. So, when that is what occurs the scripture reader can be fairly sure that it was the all-loving Father who was speaking through the words which had been read[1] and who had all the time been guiding him or her toward the life which has been promised to us all. Such people consequently will become much more inclined to plan and to make sure that they will have the necessary time for their revitalising *lectio* each day.

But there are moments on the journey when the dedicated reader finds that he or she must struggle to discover what a certain text of scripture actually means. Although a passage may be read each day and for the most part easily understood, a time will come when what is read may not make any sense at all. Then, if it is not left aside as one of those 'for tomorrow' verses, help may be required and sometimes unexpectedly supplied.

In this connection, let us call to mind the story of a strange but Bible-reading person whom I always thought of as the patron saint for all who struggle with the scriptures. He was that bewildered eunuch who was puzzled by some verses in Isaiah.[2] He apparently was pondering a text which was in front of him and wondering what it might mean when suddenly an unexpected guide appeared. It was the newly-ordained Philip whom it seems God had miraculously sent. In any case this Philip was a person who already knew the passage from Isaiah but, because he had himself experienced the mystery of Christ, he now was able to appreciate it in a new and obviously satisfying way. The eunuch on his journey had not reached that point of deeper understanding yet. However, in his heart he must have been prepared for it because, as soon as Philip had explained it to him, he both willingly and formally accepted it, then joyfully continued on his way. Although in our own case we will have heard of Christ and possibly have learnt to treasure our relationship with him, that eunuch is still able to encourage us. Does he not seem to say that it is good at times to struggle with a text of scripture and that, when we have discovered what it really means, perhaps with somebody's assistance, we will then be able to relax and to accept with confidence the way that lies ahead?

But we can overstate this need in us for outside help. Of course the scriptures do come from a century and a culture which is not our own and so, if for no other reason, we can benefit from scholars who are able to interpret them against the times in which they were composed. Moreover, as we have already seen, they can have meanings which we may not even glimpse until some other person speaks of his or her own personal experience and then we may discover unexpected ways of understanding them. But on the other hand it certainly would be a shame if all those who desired to let themselves be guided by the scriptures felt that they had always to consult the scholars or a spiritual guru or indeed the magisterium of the church. So what I am suggesting here is that we should 'go gladly to the sacred text'[3] just as a would-be tributary flows without concern towards the river which, when entered, will embrace and nourish it with all that it already has. In other words the Spirit which has guided us towards the scriptures will then help us to absorb the basic message of acceptance which all verses somehow indicate and which the all-absorbing sea when we have reached it will most certainly convince us has been true.

But meanwhile there will be occasions when we will begin to wonder, 'what comes next?' Of course the answer is we do not know, just as the river cannot see what is around the next bend of the ground. Yet, people speak to us of other rivers and suggest that some day they may meet with ours. One carries with it the Koran, the books Mohammad wrote. Another brings the wisdom of the Buddha and a third refers to that 'great person of the brightness of the sun',[4] through whom alone the one who wishes to transcend the mystery of death must go. It would be wonderful indeed if our own river could expand and welcome all the riches which those other great traditions seem to have. It will. Then everyone who has come from the same and ever-fruitful source will find that they are destined to be one in that unending sea which will continue to absorb them more and more.

But how will this take place? We do not know but certain answers are beginning to emerge as water from the catchment areas of some of those traditions trickle into ours. They bring their own particular and often very different ways of understanding life but happily a lot of people find that much of what they say and do can be enriching for themselves. However, thoughts from those traditions can do more. They can remind us of the comparable currents in our own tradition which have frequently been overlooked.[5] Indeed they can encourage us to read again and to examine in a more inclusive light those verses in the scriptures which declare that everything is held 'in Christ'[6] and that all that exists has been intended and then made for him.[7] Perhaps our river on its journey would expand more quickly if we could discover and accept what those great verses really mean.

The Tapestry

Many years ago I came across a weaver at his loom. I watched him for a while, quite fascinated as he wove his woollen threads into a tartan scarf. He had inherited a very old tradition which in previous centuries had produced not only articles of clothing, but great tapestries as well. However, at that time I did not think about the history of his trade nor did it strike me that the story which we can discover in the Bible is a kind of tapestry as well. But now it seems to me that this can be a very useful metaphor.

Let me develop this.

When people read a section of the Bible they may not at first consider it within the context of the whole. Instead they may just let the words which they have read touch something in themselves and, in so doing, find that they have been confirmed, or maybe challenged, in their own convictions and belief. That is not wrong and in the end it is what must be done. But in the meanwhile they might have a better understanding of what God is saying through those very words if they were also able to relate them to some other verses of the scriptures. Then the words which they had read would be supported by some other passages and so their deepest meaning would become much more convincing than it had been up till then.

To put that in another way: the different writers of the scriptures were aware of what a number of their predecessors had proclaimed and frequently they wove into their thoughts and writings many images and words which had been used before. To take a quick example we could note one section in the gospel of St John. In it the author wrote that Jesus had declared himself to be a light and did so to assure his readers that they would not walk in darkness if they followed him.[1] However in a footnote or a side-note to that text there well could be a reference to certain verses in the book of Exodus. So, if we were to turn the pages back, we would discover that the author of that older book had also spoken of a light, the one which led the Israelites as they were struggling through the desert to a promised land.[2] It, therefore, looks as if St John was conscious of that epic story and, attracted by the image of a guiding light, perceived that it was very relevant to what he wished to say. That was quite simply that if anyone felt threatened or confused or even lost, there was in Jesus Christ an incarnated light which could guide everyone towards an even better 'promised land'. Thus his own message was in that way reinforced and so enabled to become much more encouraging to those who heard or read it than if it had only been a single, isolated verse.

As we get used to contemplating all of scripture as a tapestry, we will begin to see that some threads which are prominent in certain places can in others vanish almost totally. For instance, let us look at those which indicate contempt or condemnation of one's enemies. They are at first quite strong and even re-appear from time to time until eventually they are superseded by another and a brighter one. Thus in the section which portrays the book of Genesis they tell us that a sevenfold revenge for wrongs had been allowed for Cain and seventy times sevenfold for somebody called Lamech.[3] Then, as we move on along our tapestry, we notice that this thread of vengeance sometimes re-appears but in a way which makes it seem less dark. It has in fact become united with a modifying one when, for example, it is said that only one eye may be taken for another and a tooth is all that may be taken for a tooth.[4] A sense of justice is beginning to creep in! However, when we contemplate that section of the tapestry which represents the gospel of St Matthew we will not see much that indicates revenge. Instead there is encouragement to love one's enemies and to forgive them, not just once or seven times, but seventy times seven times.[5] The wheel has turned. The bright new thread of charity has almost totally suppressed the impact of the darker one. Yet, while we can admire this section of the tapestry and often do, we may become aware that it is also saying something which we too may often need to hear!

The movement from revenge to love is not, however, always very smooth. The darker threads in fact can still be found in those parts of our tapestry which illustrate New Testament ideas, while on the other hand there are some places in the earlier parts in which a brighter and at times a sparkling one is seen. We find one of the latter, for example, in the section which recalls the preaching of a prophet called Hoseah. He, who lived eight hundred years before the birth of Christ, proclaimed to his contemporaries, who were in fact about to be invaded, what should certainly have been for them good news. It was that God is not a vengeful deity as many must have thought but one who is not only merciful, but also always steadfast in his love. He even told them that that love, unlike its normal human form, was so strong that it had no breaking point at all.[6] His own conviction of that truth, which must have seemed so novel at the time, came from a personal experience, that of his own enormous and unfailing love for Gomer who was his unfaithful and deserting wife. Thus did a bright if struggling thread appear quite suddenly among a lot of much more sober-coloured ones.

It is a pity that an insight of such quality and depth should have become so easily forgotten by so many when life seemed to settle down again. But that is what so frequently occurs. In our own lives, for instance, there may surely have been some occasions when we too were touched by that same sparking light of total, if apparently unreasonable, love. If so, we too would have become convinced, if only for a little while, that it was certainly the most important and most wonderful experience in all the world. But then as life went on and other forces intervened we may have tended to forget just how important that experience had been. So let us move along the tapestry because, as if to bring us back to that experience, the sparking thread will reappear again and this time to express the message of that great climatic parable, the one which speaks about a father waiting patiently for his own wayward child and happily embracing him as soon as he returns.[7] The sparkling thread will surely triumph in the end.

There are a lot of other threads which have been used by those who wrote the scriptures but to follow all of them would be an almost endless, even if rewarding, task. One can of course pursue a special one that is of interest by the use of a concordance or a book that has collected Bible themes. More easily one can pursue the references which are printed at the bottom of the Bible page or at the margin of the text. They will indeed direct us to the verses which have influenced the one that we are reading or to later ones which have been influenced by thoughts which it itself contains. Indeed if any of them is supported by an arrow or some other special sign it certainly should be investigated. It refers to places where our thread emerges in a very special and important way. But do not rush. A satisfying understanding of the tapestry of scripture can be gradually acquired by following such clues from time to time but even more so by a regular and prayerful reading of the text. Then, as a consequence, a wondrous happening will occur. The bits and pieces of our own lives will be woven into a cohesive pattern and one which, seen by other people, should in turn be helpful and encouraging for them.

However, for the moment let us go back once again to that part of our tapestry which illustrates the exodus from Egypt and the long but guided journey which continues to the so-called promised land. It tells us that God chose a people who had been oppressed and, making them his own, protected them as they went on from one oasis to the next. In later sections we shall see how many prophets used that ancient and heroic story to remind the Jewish people of their obligations to obey the God who had adopted them, but also that some other prophets used it with another and refreshing emphasis. It was to indicate to their contemporaries that God, who had done so much for their forebears, was prepared to do the same and even more for them. Thus one of those insightful prophets, whom in fact we do not know by name, proclaimed to all the Jews who had been carried into exile that their God would manifest himself again and lead them from their new oppression to the land which they so much desired.[8] In joyful words, which would be used again, he said that God was going to prepare 'a way in the wilderness'[9] as he had done before and, even if it was to be from Babylon and not from Egypt, that is what he did. So now, when we in turn perceive how those two journeys are presented, our own hopes for future happiness should be revitalised. At least the bright threads in these sections of the tapestry suggest that, even though we too at times may have to carry our own cross, there is a new Jerusalem ahead and that, when all things are made new, those who arrive there will rejoice forever more.

But let us also note one very special thread which always tries to re-assure us that our struggle is worthwhile. It is the one which indicates the person who, not only teaches us the way we have to go, but also leads us by the quality of his own dedicated life. For all the early Christians it of course was Jesus who fulfilled that role. But when we stop to see how he has been portrayed by the evangelists we will begin to notice some supporting threads which had been used before. Thus, for example, there is one which indicates that he, as son, had been called 'out of Egypt'[10] and another which declares that he spent 'forty days and forty nights' alone with God.[11] So, as we gaze admiringly at these, as we are meant to do, the memory of Moses who himself had come from Egypt and who then had spent that same amount of time with God before he led the Isrealites to their own promised land may come into our minds. If so our own conviction that we will be led by him who is an even greater Moses will be strengthened and our hope will be confirmed.

One final thought.

It is that, while this tapestry has many threads which find their own fulfilment in the life of Christ, it can be also taken as a useful mirror of our own. Indeed in it 'we see our beauty and our ugliness, our progress and the distance which we have to travel still'. So wrote St Gregory the Great[12] some sixteen centuries ago. I have already mentioned that we are not yet completely 'beautiful' when speaking of the fact that certain dark threads can remain although the shining one of love has come to dominate the scene. I have suggested on the other hand that we already have made progress when I spoke about that other thread which long before the time of Jesus had revealed the love which comes from God. So, while in this life we will always be a mixture of what both threads symbolise, the thrust of the whole tapestry of scripture gives us hope. It constantly reminds us that the Spirit-weaver will continue working until we, with multi-coloured splendour, will become what the completed tapestry would certainly portray.

The View from the Top

Not long ago I crossed the Vee. It is a scenic mountain route which leads from Tipperary into Waterford. At first it rises quickly, while below the wide expanse of rich and open countryside comes into view. Indeed some details which had not seemed very interesting before can then appear as part of an inspiring landscape which delights the gazing traveller. Then, when an even higher vantage point has been attained, one may sit down and quietly admire the whole terrain. It is the same with scripture. There are passages which may appear at first uninteresting but there are others which, when reached, may make it possible for us to see the hidden values of the ones which we had left behind. But there are also what I call 'peak verses'. They are those which let us have a glimpse of who we really are.

The first time I became aware of the dependence of some scripture verses on some others was when I was in the middle of a sharing group. The well-known passage in the gospel of St Matthew which declares that Christians should forgive, not only once or even seven times, but seventy times seven times had been both read and pondered silently. Then almost everybody spoke and said what it had meant for him or her, that is except one person who sat silently not saying anything at all. Then somebody began to read another text. It was the one which says that Jesus on the cross repeatedly exclaimed: 'Forgive them, Father, for they know not what they do.'[1] It was a providential choice because the one who up till then had been so quiet said, as if just speaking to herself: 'So that is how it can be done.' The prayer and attitude of Jesus had apparently enabled her, not just to face whatever hurt she had received, but also to perceive that they who caused it did not really understand her aspect of the situation. So, she seemed to have concluded that there was no need for her to make a daunting effort to forgive whoever had in some way wounded her and probably by then forgotten her as well. Instead she could rejoice that she was free, free to let them go and free to get on with her life. In other words the first verse by itself had made her conscious, not just of her hurt, but also of an incapacity to forgive. The second verse, however, raised her to a higher level where she could indeed perceive the hurts she had received but at the same time be inspired by one who did his best to cope with his, and seemingly with much success.

A second case, or type of case, to reinforce what I have said may also be considered here. It is concerned with the idea of love which in the first three gospels is presented in a two-fold way, that is to love the Lord our God and then to love our neighbour too.[2] But that, it could at least be argued, indicates not just a high ideal, but an ethical imperative as well. In consequence it can suggest a problem. How can one obey a law which is so open-ended that it cannot be defined? The first commandment, 'to love God', does not say how that can be satisfactorily done; the second asks what seems to be at times impossible. Indeed the fact that many people who are good will say that their prevailing fault is selfishness should give us cause to think. So what is the solution? Obviously it is either to ignore these so-called great commandments altogether or to find a formula which will allow what they imply to seem, not just attractive, but to some extent attainable as well.

So let us climb the mountainside and see if we can find a similar but more facilitating text. Perhaps one from the elevated gospel of St John will do. It also speaks of love and even says it is a new commandment but, as we reflect on it, we recognise a difference. The author has brought us into the atmosphere of what was no less than a farewell meal, and so our interest and attention are diverted from the noun to its expectant adjective. We, therefore, tend to understand this 'newness' as a parting gift which will indeed be able to affect and guide our daily lives.

To those who, from their *lectio*, are able to recall how Jeremiah had declared that in the future God would make another and a better covenant with his own people,[3] this particular gospel proclamation might suggest that what had been so long expected was at last to be accomplished. And it was. But life went on and problems came and once again the energy for loving one another tended to decline. Yet, as we now look back again on him who washed the feet of his disciples we may find, as many have, that it can also be restored.

Some scholars will at this stage urge us to ascend a little higher so that we will have an even more exhilarating view. They will, for instance, intimate that when we will have reached a certain point we will be able to perceive that 'as I have loved you' is actually causative. In other words, they tell us that the phrase should be translated as 'because I have loved you' and, if that is the case, it would make quite a difference,[4] would it not? Indeed, to take an ordinary-life experience, when anybody knows that he or she is loved by someone else, an energy can be released which almost guarantees a willing and a generous response. So when we think of all the people who were sure that Jesus gave his life for them, we should not really be surprised that they were ready to give theirs to him. In other words the more that we reflect on what the author of this elevated gospel wrote, the more we will be able to observe what was in fact implied in the abbreviated formula which we had questioned for a while. 'To love God and to love one's neighbour' was intended to be no more than just a useful summary of what the Christian life is really all about.

But there are other verses on the scripture-landscape which appear to be not on the plain or even on a fairly elevated place, but high up on the very mountain top. They are the ones which, often in symbolic ways, reveal the life to which we all are called. They are indeed 'peak verses' and, although they may appear to some as being far beyond their reach, it is important to allow our minds to be absorbed by them, especially as we will have to come down to the plain again and then to walk with many people who are groping from one situation to the next.

The story of the baptism of Jesus is, I would suggest, one of those peak or very special sections of the gospels.[5] It does not refer to going up a mountain as some others do but it reveals the same inviting mystery which the spiritual mountaineer is called to know. It is that we ourselves are loved by God and that, while what the future holds is not yet known, we can be filled with his transforming Spirit and so guided through whatever comes until we reach the life which will not ever end. There is no doubt that the evangelists believed that Jesus was unique and consequently that the wonderful experience of being loved and Spirit-filled by God would have been somewhat different for him than it would be for us. However, since he also was like us in everything but sin,[6] we can expect to share to some extent in his own peak experiences, which in fact is what he obviously wanted us to do.

The story of the baptism is, therefore, ours as well. We are the chosen ones on whom the Spirit comes and we are those whom God addresses as his own beloved ones. So if we now look back to certain moments in the past we may begin to see that even then we were being blessed by God. But what we probably did not perceive was that we were beginning to be divinised.

There is, however, one more peak or very special passage in the gospels which deserves to be considered here. It is the one which says that Jesus was transfigured and, on that occasion we can note that it fits easily into our metaphor because it did in fact occur when he was on a mountain.[7] So it clearly seems to say that anytime we leave the pressures of our daily lives behind and seek out for ourselves some quiet, even elevated, place we too may sense again that deifying mystery which we noticed when reflecting on the passage which described his baptism. In other words we may experience again the presence of the Spirit, which has been suggested by the cloud, and we may recognise again the silent voice of one who, though invisible, proclaims that we are his beloved ones. But when we read the well-known story of what happened on Mount Tabor we can strangely feel unmoved!

What can we do? We were not there with Peter, James and John when that event was happening and so we do not share the memories which could excite us as we read about or celebrate this great event. Yet it is said, particularly in the Eastern churches, that what we are celebrating in the feast of the Transfiguration is what life is really all about. Indeed the East will say that, even if we are involved in pastoral activity or in some vital ministry of mercy, what is most important is to let ourselves be saturated with the Holy Spirit just as Jesus was. We therefore must and can be divinised, and yet I often fail to feel excited as that major feastday re-appears each year. Perhaps it is because I am inclined, like many others, to expect or to ignore too much.

However, as I was reflecting on this disappointment I remembered that I too had once seen somebody who was or seemed to be transfigured. (Maybe there were others but this is the one who stands out in my mind.) The person to whom I refer was (as a lot of people might agree) quite ordinary, good – yes very good, but not perhaps what would be thought of as exceptionally so. Yet not too long before he died I saw him, suddenly and unexpectedly, in what was certainly a very different light. He was in fact not doing anything that could be thought of as extraordinary. He was simply talking to another person or, more accurately, answering some questions which were being put to him. So maybe it was I who suddenly was changed. If so the grace which I received allowed me to perceive and to admire the grace, or light, which at that moment seemed to flow through him.

I frequently have thought about that startling moment and, connecting it with the Transfiguration story which it illustrates, I have at times been struck by what is both an interesting and a consoling thought. It is that he or she who is transfigured does not know that it is so. Indeed the person whom I saw transfigured was, as I have said, just getting on with his own life and doing what seemed necessary at the time. No more! But then it was the same with Jesus. No one ever said that he was conscious that his own appearance had been altered. He was only doing what he did so often which, in this case, was to spend some quiet time with him who could and would sustain him as he faced the challenges which each day seemed to bring. So what can we conclude but that it is the privilege of others to perceive the presence and the growth of the divine in people, who have better things to do than to be conscious of themselves.

Yet such a moment can help all who have perceived it to be sure that they are also loved by God and that, if they come down to the plain again, as they will have to do, God may in turn encourage others by the light which they alone will have the privilege to see.

Prayer

If we wish to prefer a petition to men of high station,
we do not presume to do so without humility and respect;
how much more ought we to supplicate
the Lord God of all things
with all humility and devotion.
And let us be sure that
we shall be heard, not for our much speaking,
but for purity of heart and tears of compunction.
(*Rule of Benedict, chapter 20*)

Awareness

'From the greatness and the beauty of created things there comes a corresponding perception of their creator.' So wrote the writer of the Book of Wisdom[1] but have we the eyes to see? 'The world is charged with the grandeur of God', wrote Gerard Manley Hopkins,[2] but how often have we even noticed it?

The wisdom writer was upset that many people were unable, from the good things that are seen, to know the One from whom they come. Nor did they recognise the craftsman while they paid attention to his works, he went on to assert.[3] But everyone can fall into that trap. Each one can make a finite thing into a god and so become insensitive to the Greater Presence that is trying to attract us in so many different ways. Indeed when it from time to time succeeds, each one of us can easily ignore it or presume that it is less important than it is.

Do we not, therefore, often need to let our minds and hearts be purified so that they may be free to see the grandeur and the beauty and indeed the 'godness' of all things.

* * *

From where I live it takes two hours to reach the coast. But it is worth the effort and, away from all concerns, I can while driving through the countryside look forward to that final mountain bend and to my first glimpse of the sea which, as a wandering psalmist put it, is both 'vast and wide'.[4] But then, as if drawn by a magnet, I move on to find a closer vantage point where one is able to admire the strength of its successive waves and the beauty of its here or there but ever-dancing spray.

Yet when I have returned refreshed I always seem to need the city-dweller to remind me of the wonders of the place in which I actually live each day. 'The air is fresh,' one guest exclaimed, 'and the water is pure and we can see the stars.' How true! Yet even that can be so easy to forget. The God whom I perceived in wave and spray is also found at home.[5]

* * *

Miles away from everybody's dwelling place there is a quiet spot where all the thoughts and feelings which accumulate each day can fade and then begin to find in their proper places in the store-house of our memories. For Benedict that spot was Subiaco, 'a deserted place' some forty miles from Rome and, according to the story which has been passed down, he stayed there as a hermit for some years.[6] As time went on it seems that all the pressures and the superficial pleasures of his past life slid into his long-term memory. Of course new worries and distractions surfaced in the silence, that is true, and these came to him more directly, and aggressively, from elements that are in fact within us all and which need to be named and tamed. But Benedict by the grace of God 'came to himself',[7] the most important dwelling place of all. He consequently found that he was able to continue doing what he knew he should and so become progressively aware of simply being in the presence of the 'Lord God of all things'.[8]

We touch here on what obviously was a very deep experience and one which often can do so much more than can those shorter periods of 'quiet time' which many people seek at regular, and even daily, intervals. These 'desert moments' or, as might be said within the Celtic world, these 'dysart' moments, are more searing but they tend to be more focusing as well. They, therefore, need to be remembered, and not just because what happens during them can often re-enforce what happens to us in those ordinary 'quiet times', but also to remind us of the course that we are on.

Surprise
I remember coming home one autumn night and seeing, in the downward beam from my bicycle-lamp, the multi-coloured leaves which lay along the road. It was a magic moment and although a lot of decades have since then passed by, I can recall it still.

A psalmist who lived centuries ago looked up one night at a starry sky and felt not only admiration and indeed a sense of awe, but also, in comparison, that complementary sense of being very small.[9] Today when we in turn gaze up we may remember hearing that our little planet 'earth' on which we stand is but a piece of rock which travels round the outside of what is itself no more than just one galaxy among innumerable more. No wonder then that we at such a time can feel amazed and almost insignificant. Perhaps that psalmist whom I mentioned could be said to have personified us all when he exclaimed to God: 'Oh what are we, mere mortals, that you keep us in your mind?'

These moments have been isolated but each one of us no doubt has his or her own album of such wonder-memories. They are worthwhile revisiting because they can prepare us for the ones which are to come.

Surprise.

It does not have to be a visual event. It could be something which we taste or smell or touch or hear. I think of certain people who have said that they can still remember such a homely and consoling moment as the unexpected flavour of a meal or maybe the relaxing scent of many a garden flower. I also think of how an elderly lady who, with understandable regret, said 'no one wants to touch me any more' and then discovered to her great relief that her conclusion was not true. Perhaps that later made it possible for her to know the thrill, which others can so easily have, that of becoming conscious of, and then uplifted by, the singing of a nearby bird.

What can we do in situations such as these except to let ourselves relax and then rejoice and with a song in our own hearts to make our contribution to the total, cosmic offering of praise.

* * *

The icon
I have one in my room. It may not be a very ancient one but it is striking and impressive. It expresses in a graphic way a presence which is everywhere.

AWARENESS

I have been told that long ago when iconographers were asked to make an icon for a church or for a private person they would get a board of wood and quietly prepare it. Then when it was ready, and when they were ready too, they would apply the gold or gold-leaf. That was not a form of paint, although that would be later often used, but the shining and metallic sign of the divinity itself. The person to be re-presented then was, as it were, brought forth from that rich background of eternal light and so a saint or Christ himself appeared. Indeed in one particular icon which I know the golden light seems to be percolating through the person there portrayed, and has in fact become apparent on the vestments which that person wears. So one can say, as I quite often do, 'this is an icon of a certain saint but it is also that particular person being divinised'. The value of that statement is that it allows me to continue with the comment, 'so are you who pray in front of it'.

The second letter of St Peter has already told us that we are 'partakers in the divine nature'[10] and St Paul expressed that thought with great vitality when, writing to the church at Corinth, he declared that 'we are being changed from one degree of glory to the next'.[11] The eastern Christians were attracted by that divinising thought and spoke of it in different ways. Indeed, as we can see, they even let it manifest itself, not only through their icons, but also in the way in which those icons were themselves produced.

So to return to mine, I know that it contains a presence which is very real and able to affect and even divinise me as I turn to it with reverence and pray. To say that it is just a 'holy picture' can be, therefore, quite inadequate, although it is a picture and although the person who has been portrayed on it can be considered holy. To refer to it as 'representing' someone is unsatisfactory too, although we would come closer to what many people feel if that verb were to be considered in a hyphenated way. Yet to assert that such a saint or even Christ himself is 're-presented' in the icon, or indeed in 'holy pictures' which are found in many private homes, would still fall short of the perceived reality. Then 'what words can we use?', some one might ask, or 'does the world in which we live no longer have the categories of thought which can express what we believe?' There, in that second question lies the problem which we often have. Yet, while our power of reason will inevitably fail, our intuition keeps on telling us that Christ or some particular saint is present in the icon or the image which we have. It therefore can and will, if we agree, bring us 'from one degree of glory to the next', that is into the deifying light[12] which has been promised to us all.

***

'And God made humankind in his own image and likeness.'[13] There it is, a basis for the many statements which proclaim our human dignity and, in consequence, our human rights. Whatever terms like image and likeness may imply, the basic truth is that each person is essentially a manifestation of the One from whom all good things come.

The second story of creation speaks about this in its own and storytelling way. It tells us that the breath, that is the life, which everybody has is a participation in the life of God. The Lord God formed man of dust from the ground and breathed into him the breath of life and man became a living being.[14] As the woman had not yet been made, at least according to this chapter, and because when that occurred she was referred to as being taken from his side, we can presume the obvious. That is that for the author she too shares in that God-given dignity which he has said that man already had. In any case, and leaving controversial thoughts aside, she too, with him, is part of God's self-manifestion here on earth.

However, it is also true that men and women do not always seem to be as perfect as such statements would suggest. Indeed the sacred scriptures constantly remind us of our human failings and our faults and even of our pain in being far from what our deepest selves desire. But taken as a whole they balance this by indicating that, if we are not that perfect image/likeness now, with God's continuous and constantly repeated help that is what we are able to become.

So meanwhile 'godness' can in many ways seep through us all and those who can perceive it may discover that, as Benedict declared, the most unlikely person can be sent by God to help them to improve. Moreover 'love', which is one name for God, may flow through many people in a lot of different ways and those who welcome it will find that, thanks to them, they can develop as they should. In all such helping and facilitating people God's own Spirit will be present and at work and so those people will be, for a time at least, no less than God's anointed ones for us.

For that, as we discover it, we surely should give thanks.

***

AWARENESS

It seems to me as if all things, and people too, are parts of one great cosmic symphony.

That was a kind of vision that I had in student days. I liked it and, reflecting on what it implied, I would perceive with definite delight that everything, and everyone, makes his or her or its own special contribution to what surely is to be a masterpiece. So what both fascinated and inspired me most was the apparent beauty which the harmony of all was able to produce.

As I became aware of what that vision meant, it turned out to be useful in two different but ultimately connected ways. It helped me, for example, to approach the subject I was studying, not as a dry collection of specific thoughts, but as a living part of God's creation which was making its own contribution to the whole. Indeed it helped me to relate to people too because, no matter who they were or how I felt about them, it associated them directly with the God whose Spirit was in some way living in and breathing through each one of them. It consequently even made provision for what often seemed to be discordant notes or strange or misplaced melodies. Indeed although at times I may have wondered if such seeming aberrations could have any useful part to play at all, this image would repeatedly assure me that all would be well.[15] The Great Conductor knew what he was doing and was able to develop every melody so that the role of each within the whole would at the end be clearly recognised.

My own awareness through this insight, therefore, was, not only of an unseen Maestro who would bring in every instrument at the appropriate time but also, as I have suggested, of his Spirit which is breathing in each one of us. That means, of course, that it must breathe through me as well! I too am called to play a part in the production of the still unfinished symphony.

Loving Words

If relationships can blossom in a fruitful silence, as they can, there are occasions when it certainly is good to speak. A word well chosen, for example, can express the wish, not only to communicate, but also to become united with another. That is true in human friendships and it is no less so in the case of a relationship with God.

However, let us note that when we speak to anyone as to a friend we do so to a person whom we have already known. So, if we speak to God as to a friend, we will be doing so from our own personal experience of how he has revealed himself to us. I am implicitly referring here to past events in our own lives in which his wisdom or his goodness had been active in some special and decisive way. I am implicitly referring too to those significant people who were at the time a part of our own lives and who are consequently shining through our memories still. They are the ones who made it possible for us to trust and love that great self-giving One from whom they ultimately came.

For those who diligently ponder scripture I am able to extend this pattern and thereby to remind them of a basic fact which they, no doubt, will have discovered for themselves. It is that God is one who always wants to help whoever may be in distress and who desires to share his joy and even his own life with everyone. This was in different ways revealed to all the chosen people through the presence and the words of those who were themselves, at least eventually, recognised as having being the great prophetic people of their race. It then was obvious in a very special way through him who laid down his own life in order that all those who followed him could live. Thus, strengthened by the knowledge of this constantly repeated revelation of God's self-donating presence in our lives, our own response can always veer towards a word of gratitude, which may at times imply as well not less than the total offering of ourselves.

A point worth noting here, however, is that, as in every intimate relationship, the word or words which we employ in prayer will frequently be personal and even very private ones. Did not the great Teresa once proclaim that, when the soul has striven to cut down the ramblings of the intellect and has become aware of just being in the presence of the God who gives himself to us, then all that it desires to do is express some 'loving words'?[1] How good, indeed how wise, of her not to suggest, much less impose, some formula which she may have found useful for herself. She obviously wanted her own readers to relax and to allow their own words to emerge and then to carry them to him. Such words, whatever they may be, will consequently be worthwhile remembering and, in the days to come, repeating in the heart so that they may again bring our own inmost selves to him who loved us first.

A second point worth noting is that our own 'loving words', although in one sense very private, may not in themselves be very different from those which other people tend to use in similar situations. They may even have been borrowed, more or less unconsciously, from the writings or the sayings of another. Thus some people have, at least at times, desired to read and make their own some prayer which was composed by some particular saint; while others, for example, have been drawn to ponder prayerfully the verses of a psalm and then to make their sentiments their own. This latter practice was, perhaps, the way which had been used by the disciples of St Benedict himself. He certainly suggested in his Rule that they should put aside some time each day to study them so that, when they assembled for their daily liturgies, their mind and hearts might be more easily in harmony with their voices.[2] So it is not too unlikely, then, that anytime they wished to pray alone they would have quietly recalled some of those verses which they knew so well and then allowed the words which they contained to mould and carry their own thoughts and sentiments to God. Indeed, just sitting still and quietly repeating certain verses from a chosen psalm could have disposed them both to focus their distracted minds and consequently to allow their spirits to relax within the all-embracing mystery of the One whom they invoked.

Thus maybe some of those who used the psalms for their own private prayer would have discovered that a verse such as 'I thank you Lord for you have heard the cry of my appeal,'[3] could keep them going for a while. It is indeed a loving line and full of deep-felt gratitude. However, while this is a verse which has a very strong appeal, there is another one which certainly became a favourite among the very early monks and has had repercussions down the ages to this present time. It is the one in which the psalmist cried out for some help. 'O God, come to my aid, O Lord, make haste to help me.'[4] I imagine that it could have been quite frequently recalled and quietly repeated when life was becoming tedious or difficult. No wonder then that it became the opening verse for almost every section of the church's prayer. So, maybe it, as well as the thanksgiving one which I have mentioned, could be added profitably to the repertoire of anyone who is inspired to use the ancient psalms for his or her own personal response to God.

For those who are attracted to this psalm-involving way of prayer, it may be useful to pass on a tip which was passed on to me. It is that, if one has a psalm-book or a leaflet that contains some verses, one should read each line as if it were an item on a menu. Each in fact has been prepared with care and, down the ages, tried and polished and, moreover, has been found by many people to contain a flavour of its own. But then, when we have spent some time with each suggestion on the menu, we may find that our own eyes are constantly returning to the one which has attracted us the most. That is the one to choose and then to sit with and enjoy. We can digest it slowly and indeed, not only there and then, but also in a quiet way throughout the hours which are to come. It will provide for us the stimulating nourishment we need.

Each person prays however in his own, or her own, very special way and so each one of us has to discover which particular prayer-word is the one which can help us the most. If I have spoken of the possibility of using verses from a psalm it is because this is a route which has attracted many. But it certainly is not the only one, and so some mention much be made here of at least the so-called 'Jesus Prayer'. This was already known, and obviously used, before the end of the first Christian century and we can find it in its Aramaic form, 'Maranathá', in certain parts of the New Testament itself.[5] Then later it developed from the simple, 'Come, Lord Jesus' to the formula, 'Lord Jesus Christ have mercy on me, a sinner.' If this more extended formula was used at certain times within the Eastern churches in a very systematic way, what may be of particular interest here is that a lot of prayerful people in the West have recently discovered that some version of this 'Jesus Prayer' can be for them a most effective way to union with the One whom their own inmost selves desire.

Here, however, all I want to say about this 'Jesus Prayer' is that, unlike the psalms, it is addressed explicitly, not to the Father, but to Christ. That might appear to narrow its appeal, not just to Christians, but to those who like to focus their attention on a person whose humanity they can admire. But on the other hand, if Christ is seen not only as a person who can help us on our way, but also as the one in whom the fullness of God was pleased to dwell,[6] this need not be the case. Indeed those who discover that this kind of prayer can be for them the 'loving words' which they require, may find that in addressing him who is the Christ they are in fact transcending human limitations and becoming one with the divine which was and is revealed especially in him. In other words, the Spirit brings them through those words, and through the Word, to him who thereby draws them to himself.

But it is easy to forget that such a One is really present everywhere, and always yearning to make us more Christ-like in our own relationship with him. So in our often busy lives we frequently will have to make an effort if we are to keep in contact with that God who, while beyond all definitions, never ceases to desire to come into our ordinary lives. That effort may, however, be reduced if we have found some 'prayer-words' which have in the past expressed our own reaction to that Presence when we have become aware of it. To quietly retrieve them may in turn remind us that there is a Presence when perhaps it had seemed for a while that there was none. Indeed, to use a telling metaphor, to say a chosen prayer-word can be similar to turning an ignition key, while to repeat it gently and from time to time may help to keep the spiritual petrol flowing and, in consequence, allow us to make progress on our journey towards the One in whom alone we can be totally fulfilled.

As our relationship with this all-loving God and Father grows, our motives for responding to him will no doubt begin to change. This is of course the kind of growth which will take place in all relationships if they develop well. At first our motives, more or less disguised, may be to some extent to have the consolations which the saying of some loving words can easily dispose us to expect. But later, as our own awareness of the dignity and independence of the other starts to grow, our motive is more likely to allow the loved one to become what he or she is meant and called to be. Such a development of our intentions may of course be only gradual and certainly it will include the overcoming of much selfishness, but God is good and often helps us to achieve it through the changing and at times demanding circumstances of our lives. So in the context of the ultimate relationship, that is of that which is between God and ourselves, the 'loving words' which nurture it will come in time to indicate a willingness, not to possess, but to adore. They will as well include the will to let oneself be used in such a way that no one will be hindered by us from receiving all the life which God, the loving animator, has in store for everyone.

The world out there, however, often seems to run on principles of its own. That is from one perspective how it ought to be. Yet the political and economic forces which are so apparent are not always quite as fundamental as they seem. Indeed investigation shows, and has in many cases shown, that they are often only secondary to the human forces which in fact determine everything. So, when all has been said and done, the memorable words of what was once a well-known song were nearer to the truth than many of its singers may have ever realised. In any case they happily proclaimed that it is 'love which makes the world go round'. If that in fact is how it is, then our own most urgent task is to make sure that we unselfishly absorb into ourselves the most unselfish strand of love because it is the one which, paradoxically, is the most effective one. Our 'prayer-words' therefore, may become at times that totally self-giving one which is 'thy will be done'. That will imply, not wanting to possess whoever and whatever comes our way, but to be ready to acknowledge their intrinsic dignity while gratefully accepting the transforming, if at times demanding, Spirit of the One who does not ever cease to draw us to himself.

An Underlying Quality

Benedict, when speaking about prayer, used what is today an almost unknown term. It was 'compunction'. What is that? The English dictionary tells us that it is a 'pricking of the conscience' and, for those who want to follow up its etymology, it points them to the fact that it derives from that same Latin root from which the word, or verb, 'to puncture' also comes. So if one can imagine for a moment an impressive car which has been travelling easily but then picks up a nail or piece of glass and phizz! – one can have quite a good idea of what compunction meant for those who used it when it was in vogue. It was to be deflated by some incident. But let us note that there were two quite different, if connected, types of situation which were able to effect this, certainly uncomfortable, yet often therapeutic, state.

Of these two causes of compunction one is certainly the knowledge that one has behaved in ways which were not good and so regrettable. The conscience had indeed been pricked. The other possible cause is, not from something that had happened in the past, but from our understanding of what is to come. That was for many of the older writers no less than the ever-satisfying presence of the One who would envelop them with his unending joy. So, whether one is conscious of past sins or not, the deep awareness that can come in prayer of all that is being offered to us can at times cause all of us to have a sense of infinite unworthiness. Then we may for a while experience a gentle pain but one which can, as we accept it, stimulate us to return that love as much as that is possible.

The basic elements in our relationship with God have certain counterparts in our relationships with one another. So perhaps we should give some consideration to 'compunction moments' in the human situations which for many may be more familiar. They may help us both to recognise and to appreciate the healing value of what can deflate us when we think of our relationship with God.

Some of these more recognisable 'compunction moments' may be the result of knowing with regret that in the past we had been inconsiderate or in some way impatient with another. They could certainly have come from an awareness that we had been quite unjust, or even most immoral, in the manner in which we had treated someone whom we met. However, even if we always had behaved impeccably, a feeling of 'compunction' can be caused in us by knowing that we simply are not able to relate to someone whom we love as well as he or she deserves or as our yearning hearts desire. In all such moments we can feel, not only pierced by our inadequacies, but deflated by their memory as well.

But, staying with these human situations, let us check their other and more hopeful side. It is the one which can assure us that, if handled well, our wounded or apparently impossible relationships may find a formula which will permit a new beginning and a reasonable growth. Of course some help or some encouragement from someone else may be at times required and, if we seek it, we will find it either among people whom we know or in the wise words of some authors whom we have the opportunity to read. In any case, to cope with our deflating moments will involve accepting and admitting our own weaknesses, but that itself can often introduce a touch of healthy realism into a relationship which might not have been there before. It certainly may make it possible for us to be perceived by others, not as some kind of a 'super-type', which is how we may like to see ourselves, but as the persons who we really are. This new degree of self-acceptance may in turn allow our would-be friends to understand what they should really do or be for us and then we may discover that, in spite of our deficiencies we can at last respond with confidence renewed.

It is the same with our relationship with God. We can at first pretend to be what we are not. Then as we keep on asking him for this or that or something else, what can he do but smile and wait until the situation changes and we then begin to recognise and to articulate our real and sometimes urgent needs? Indeed just as a doctor cannot give the medicine a patient needs as long as he or she refuses to admit to any problem, so too we will not be able to receive from God all that he wants to give when there is some pretence in our relationship with him. But when a puncture happens, howsoever it is caused, then the person with a problem can be forced to name it and, perhaps with some encouragement, to yearn and even pray for something more important than what he or she had previously wanted. So the healing and facilitating Spirit that God wishes to bestow may consequently be at last both given and received. Then within the context of both openness and honesty a genuine relationship with him from whom that Spirit comes will have its opportunity to grow.

I have already spoken of the psalms so let them illustrate for us this kind of situation too.

The first one I will mention is about a person who had been preoccupied by something wrong that he had done but which he had not ever spoken of to anybody else. The car had struggled on! The cancer kept developing within! 'I kept it secret and my frame was wasted', he declared.[1] Then in the end it all became too much for him and he was forced by true compunction to confess his hidden fault. We could, in passing, note that he had obviously found some person to whom he could talk and who was able to assure him that all could and would be well. So what he had kept bottled up within himself was out and happiness, no doubt with much relief, returned as he discovered that, despite his fault, he was in fact accepted by the one whom he had trusted and, because of that, he knew that God accepted him as well.

The classic case of someone who was 'punctured' by the memory of something wrong that he had done is certainly, however, that which seems to be expressed in the famous 'miserere psalm'.[2]

That is the one which starts by crying out: 'O God, have mercy on me in your kindness; in compassion blot out my offence.' Tradition tells us that these were the words of David, that great powerful king, when life for him was starting to unravel. Even though he had achieved a lot both for himself and for his people he had come to see that his misfortunes, which were many, were the consequence of having sinned. He had in fact designed a way in which the husband of the beautiful Bethsheba would be killed so that he then could take her for himself.[3] That had been wrong. He had abused his own position to achieve what was not right and now because he had been driven from his throne he was not able to eradicate the memory of that offence. 'My sin is always there before me,'[4] he bewailed. What could he do? In fact he had no choice but to accept responsibility and then, perhaps with help from some prophetic and inspiring friends, to hope with growing confidence that God would cure his wounds and bless him once again.

Our most important model for compunction is of course the first of the apostles, Peter, who had wanted to be so committed but who failed so miserably when the time of testing came. He had told Jesus that he would not ever leave him but, when pressures came a little later, he denied that he had ever even known him.[5] That was bad, and not long afterwards he came to recognise with pain that he had selfishly betrayed a friend to whom he owed so much. It may be interesting for us to note that that offence of his was the expression of a weakness which had shown itself before when Jesus had referred to all the opposition and the sufferings which were to come. On that occasion Peter, suddenly reacting, had declared that he did not want Jesus to be captured and then put to death because, of course, he knew that if that was to happen he might also be subjected to the same. In any case, what Jesus said in answer to his protestations, 'get behind me, Satan,'[6] must have wounded him because it made him recognise how selfish he had been. But now, when in the courthouse in Jerusalem 'the Lord turned round and looked at him', he certainly was very punctured and on that occasion it was by the love which he perceived. The consequence was that 'he went out and wept bitterly.'[7]

However, those were healing tears. Indeed, already as they were being shed they may have given Peter some release from his distress and certainly they paved the way for the renewal and indeed improvement of the friendship which he had enjoyed till then. But first, according to St John, he had to re-assert his love three times[8] to counteract his triple treachery and that may certainly have helped to steady him because from what we know about his later life, it seems to have been one of loyal and unblemished gratitude. The memory of his own faults and failings would however stay and keep him conscious of his weakness and his own unworthiness. But on the other hand the totally forgiving love which he received was able to sustain him in the certain hope that, even though it would be always more than he deserved, there would be much more love and happiness to come.

But let us now return to Benedict.

He speaks, not just of praying with compunction, but of cultivating it as well. The chapter in his Rule concerning Lent declares that during it his readers 'should apply themselves to prayer with tears, to reading, to compunction of heart'.[9] From that remark it is quite obvious that he was ready to allow his own disciples to become aware of their own faults and failings in relation to the God to whom they prayed. However he was certainly not advocating any superficial self-degrading nor the morbid pondering of sins and sinfulness. Such practices in fact would only have impeded his disciples from the one thing which he recommended, that of 'looking forward with the joy of spiritual longing to the holy feast of Easter'[10] and to all that that implied. So we can say that Benedict was more concerned with what is still to come than with whatever may have happened in the past, and so compunction was for him connected with not having and possessing yet all that for which we have been made.

So what can we say now about our prayer? Well, first that it will grow in unison with our acceptance of ourselves. Then, like the author of that famous 'miserere psalm', we too may have to be convinced that, even though the memory of sins committed in the past may sometimes haunt our minds, God will not 'cast us from his presence nor deprive us of his promised Holy Spirit'.[11] Then, like Peter who experienced the healing and indeed the loving presence of the One whom he had never really ceased to seek, we too may have to learn to say: 'Yes, Lord, you know I love you' or, when in a passive mood, to welcome quietly and gratefully his Spirit into ours. Then we may silently experience within ourselves a foretaste of that perfect happiness which has been promised to us all.

Trinitarian Reality

Prayer begins in God and then returns.

Most people would consider that when they are praying it is something they themselves are actually doing. In a sense they are correct but at the same time that is not the total truth. God is involved in everything. So we are able to conclude that he provides the grace which makes us want to say the prayer we say and, therefore, that our prayer when it is said is the effect of his activity as well as of our own. However, let us think a little more about this simple, if perhaps surprising, statement in a way which will allow us to appreciate the richness and indeed security that it implies.

The first and most profound thing to be said is that the movement into which we are inserted when we pray is no less than that of the Trinity itself. Thus, to re-formulate what I have said above: it starts as the all-loving Father sends his Spirit into us – and then continues as that Spirit animates our own and consequently causes us to reach out to that Father who accepts the prayer we make because of course it was originally inspired by him. The role of Christ in this will have to be, at least to some extent, examined too but first let us note well that, even though we may not always feel that it is doing any good at all, there is a definite infallibility in prayer.

Yet there are problems which we have to face. For instance if our prayers are so caught up within the movement of the Trinity why is it that so many of them seem to be unanswered? Then, accepting that our prayers are somehow part of that all-powerful movement, we might ask how anybody could say that they themselves have any choice at all or that their prayers have any value in themselves. However, as we might suspect, such questions as they stand are difficult, if not impossible, to answer. So, if we desire to handle them, what we must surely do is to perceive a context in which they will seem no longer even necessary.

Let us start, however, by considering how Luke, who had a special interest in this subject, wrote about the prayer of Jesus. He on one occasion wrote that when 'rejoicing in the Holy Spirit' he 'gave thanks' to God, his Father, for revealing so much to all those who had accepted him.[1] So we can say that that evangelist perceived, not just that Jesus as a person prayed to One whom he acknowledged as his Father, but that as he did his prayer came, not from him alone, but also from the Spirit which that Father had sent down on him. In other words he saw him in the context of that prayerful and inclusive pattern which I have just described. It would of course be interesting to speculate as to how much all that was also a projection of his own experience. No doubt to some extent it was. One fact is sure. It is that Luke himself seems to have recognised that pattern for prayer which in the opening paragraphs I have attempted to described.

However, as we read the gospel story we will sense that Jesus, like St Luke himself no doubt, had his own disappointments when his hopes did not materialise. We will moreover recognise that even Jesus at the end of his own life felt that he was deserted by the God in whom he had put all his trust and desolate because all he had done seemed to have been to no avail. So once again the kind of questions which I have suggested raise their heads and challenge us to face them and to struggle to discover even the beginnings of a satisfying answer.

Let me, therefore, start by speaking about someone who approached me many months ago. He was distressed and worried and he even asked me one of those particular questions, namely: why was his continuous prayer, which was to be released from some affliction, never answered? As he spoke of his predicament, I noted, and with some surprise, that he did not make any reference to the well-known verse in Matthew's gospel, 'ask and you will then receive,'[2] although that certainly would have been very relevant to what he had been saying. On the contrary he quoted one from Mark which reads, 'I tell you, therefore, everything you ask and pray for, just believe you have it and it will be yours.'[3] That choice was interesting, not least because it actually complicated his position by suggesting that the Father (though the word he used was 'God') did not give him what he desired because his faith (whatever that implied for him) was weak and insufficient. For a while I listened to what he was saying, yet not knowing how best to respond.

However as he talked about his problem and his life I came to recognise one detail that suggested what should happen next. It was that, like so many people, he was not unconscious of the fact that he was trying to ignore a deeper and more urgent need within himself while asking God for what in fact was no more than a superficial one. Indeed it seemed to me quite likely that what he was actually praying for, that is release from worry about certain circumstances of his life, might actually come to him if he would only just allow the Father to respond to his more fundamental one. So rather than agree that God is really unaffected by whatever prayers we make, as he apparently had done, I knew what I was able to at least suggest. It was that as a Father, God prefers to wait until the one who prays is ready both to ask for and receive the greater grace which he or she in fact so urgently requires.

But, while my comment may have helped that person at the time, another person might have pushed the argument by asking what I have in fact proposed as an alternative, although more penetrating, question. 'How can prayer have any value, if we are in fact within a movement of the Spirit which comes from the Father into us and then on its return brings us to him?' What can one say to that? Indeed it is a question which, if we accept it as it is, can force us into a dilemma. Either we will have to totally agree that everything depends on us and so conclude that God is virtually irrelevant or, on the contrary, we will have to say that everything that happens is the consequence of what the unseen and almighty God has willed and pre-ordained. However, while there obviously is some truth in both of these, what we must really do is to transcend the narrowness, and the futility of rational debate and seek instead an answer through a wider and a more inclusive route. Perhaps the one which flows from our own personal experience of love!

The person who for me had reached that point and from it offered the most satisfying answer to this problem is that now well-known and well-liked medieval mystic, Julian of Norwich. She, who was so stunningly convinced that God is Love, wrote for the benefit of all her 'even-Christians' who were often weighted down with the worries and the miseries of what was certainly a horrifying age. With kindness born of the conviction that 'all will be well,'[4] she told those who must frequently have wondered if their prayers for help had any value in the sight of God that 'we can ask our Lover anything we wish.'[5] That certainly may have astounded them! But it was uttered from within the context of a love-relationship with God and from the strong conviction that, if anyone knows that he or she is loved by him, then he or she will sooner or later always ask for what that never-failing Lover wants to give.

This is indeed a central and consoling insight but it is not in itself the final one. Like Julian and many others who throughout the ages knew that they were deeply loved, we too can learn how true it is that our response to whosoever loves us always is, if genuine, initiated by a power which is in fact much greater than our own. It is indeed in every case no less than that of the accepted spirit of the lover which possesses and enables ours to yearn and strive for union with the one from whom it comes. So in the case of our relationship with the divine and ever-loving Father it is his out-reaching Spirit which is constantly disposing and then leading us through our desires into an ever-greater unity with him. In consequence our prayer is always in the context which can be considered trinitarian.

But there is one more point that is important and worth noting here. It is that, as we journey on towards the One who calls us, we can always look to those who journey with us for support and consequently we will sometimes ask them to remember us when they themselves are praying to the Father who awaits us all. Of course the individuals whom we will normally approach for such a favour will be those who seem to us to be more open to the guiding Spirit and so better able to absorb our prayers into their own. Of those, however, it both could and should be noted that the one who from the very early days of Christianity has been perceived as able, even fore-ordained, to do this most effectively is he who consequently was considered as 'the Christ'. So when we say that our own prayers are trinitarian it is because they are, not only in themselves expressions of the Spirit which God sends into our hearts, but also – and in consequence of that – united with the perfect prayer of Christ with whom the Father is forever pleased.

There is, let it be said, not anything that is completely new in all of this. It is the faith-tradition which has been passed down the centuries. However, it is easy to forget it and to slide into a situation in which God appears to be no more than One who is 'out there' – and to whom we at times may offer certain prayers. Then, when whatever prayers we make appear to us to be unanswered, God may seem no more than just a distant Being who is more or less irrelevant to our own daily lives and, finally, as no more that the figment of a primitive imagination. That in fact is how the western world has moved throughout the last few centuries. Yet modern and thought-advancing people like Carl Jung have stated that the human being is by nature a religious animal and that it is through our religion that we find a meaning for our lives. So maybe it would not be out of step for us to both revisit and reclaim our rich inheritance and consequently to relax within that movement which is trinitarian – and able to transform us all into what we from all eternity are called to be.

* * *

The liturgy can often help us here. Although some prayers within it are addressed to Christ, the great majority are offered to the Father, with Christ being recognised as one through whom our prayer are said. Indeed to study them and, in particular, to spend time with the Eucharist Prayers, can be a valuable exercise.

They can encourage us to do what they suggest, that is let the Spirit come, not only on the bread and wine, but also on ourselves. Then we will be transformed from one degree of glory to the next[6] and so become with many others part of that one body which is the extended Christ. So how then could it be that our own prayers and we ourselves would not be welcomed and accepted by the One to whom all honour and glory is always due for ever and for ever?

The Spirit and the Bride

Spirit-filled
She ponders in her heart
The Word,
That ancient Word
Spoken long ago
But now
In fertile virgin soil
Conceived.

Sprit-filled
And yearning for her spouse
She dares
To utter now
Her word,
The word which makes them one:
The Spirit and the bride say
'Come'.

Work

The point I want to make is that our work
by its very nature,
draws us closer to God
and is
for us individually immensely beneficial.
I am simply saying that each moment of the day
provides an opportunity for us
to come closer to God.
A difficulty, a problem, is not, as it may at first seem,
a stumbling-block,
It is a stepping stone on our way to God.
(Basil Hume)

Work – A Benedictine Insight

The Rule of Benedict does not say much about the element of work.

Of course work would have been a normal feature of the life of the community which Benedict both founded and facilitated and for whom he wrote his famous Rule. The clues he gives us there about the type of work which took place at his monastery suggest that for the most part they were fairly ordinary. For example there was kitchen-work, then there was caring-work for those monks who were elderly or sick and also caring-work, though of another kind, for visitors and guests. We also know that there were craftsmen in the monastery because they are the subject of a chapter in the Rule and sometimes it would seem the whole community was asked to help in gathering the harvest from the fields. No doubt, with some imagination, we might add some other occupations to that very ordinary and domestic list. However, there were differences too between the kind of work which would have taken place in Benedict's community of fifteen hundred years ago and that of any group today and these should also be acknowledged. But my first and most important task is to suggest how all of us who are involved in any kind of work can be encouraged and inspired by the wisdom of St Benedict.

The first point I would like to make is that, when Benedict referred to work, he did so in the context of a three-point programme which he laid out as the order for each day. So let me quote from chapter 48: 'The brethren must be occupied at stated hours in manual labour and again at other hours in sacred reading.' There we find the second element which he desired his followers to incorporate into their lives each day, not only work but reading too! The first of these it could be said would have been nearly always manual; the second, one that of its very nature would engage the mind. We will have to address the fact that work today for many people can be also intellectual. That does create a certain kind of problem which we must at least make some attempt to solve. But first there is another element which Benedict does not want us to overlook.

This third and final element, the most important one of all, is prayer. In chapter 43 St Benedict declared: 'As soon as the signal of the divine office had been given, let them (the monks) abandon what they have in hand and assemble with the greatest speed, yet soberly. Let nothing therefore be put before the Work of God.' This 'Work of God' was Benedict's way of speaking of the daily prayer of his community. It was composed of psalms and readings from the scriptures and contained as well some special hymns and a concluding prayer. It consequently was quite similar to what is found today in the official 'Prayer Book of the Church'. However we could note in this connection that he also made provision in his Rule for those who wished to stay on after the conclusion of one of the 'offices' in order to digest the words which had been said or just to spend some time there praying privately. I will say something later about how this fundamental element of prayer can often influence the work we do. But now I only want to stress again how Benedict desired to organise a life which would be based on a solid three-point system. Or to put that in another way, just as a stool stands well when it is on three legs, so Benedictine life was organised by him to be sustained, not just by work, but also by the other elements of daily *lectio* and prayer.

So what can we conclude from that? Perhaps that it might be

of use if we were to evaluate our lives against this primary pattern of the Benedictine Rule. But, as I have already mentioned, there are certain differences between the life which was envisaged by the Rule and life as it is often lived today. So let me make a special reference to two of these, as they present a challenge to all those who want to benefit from the balance which the three-fold pattern of the Rule provides.

The first is that for many people work is now less manual than it used to be and that of course has had both good and not-so-good results. One of the not-so-good ones is that those whose work is only from the head are probably less rooted in the rhythm of creation and of nature than their forebears used to be. They consequently tend to be much less attuned to light and darkness, to the change of seasons and, perhaps the most important of them all, to the delay between the planting of the seed and harvest time. So what? Well, let me just observe that, if a person thinks that he or she belongs to such a 'deprived' category, it might be a good idea for him or her to start including certain elements of manual activity into the pattern of daily work and so restore some of the balance which was lost. In fact some people who design retreat days with the Benedictine Rule in mind will always plan some periods each day when only manual work is to be done.

A second difference between our lives and those of people in St Benedict's community is that for them most work took place within the area in which they lived. We read in chapter 66: 'The monastery if possible should be arranged so that all necessary things, such as water, mill, garden and various crafts may be within the enclosure.' Consequently, it was easier for those who lived in his community to dovetail work with periods of *lectio* and prayer. Today, however, many people have to travel quite a distance to their place of work and that takes time and energy. That makes it much more difficult to cater for those other elements which Benedict considered so important and which can, as we will later see, have an important and a valuable influence on the work we have to do. But in this kind of situation is there anything that can be reasonably done? Perhaps. While those who want to unify their lives will obviously have to work out their own personal solution to this problem, I am tempted to remark that it might be a good idea to check with other people who desire to do the same. In doing so they might receive not just encouragement but also practical advice.

Those, however, who do not have any choice but to be absent from their primary communities may find some consolation from the fact that even Benedict discovered that he had to make provision for that kind of situation too. Thus in his chapter 50 we can read: 'If any brothers be at work at a great distance, so that they cannot get to the Oratory at any of the proper times ... let them perform the Work of God in that place where they have been working. Let them bend their knees in reverence before God.' So simply, 'make an effort, do your best; use well-known words and even gestures too'. How feasible that is for all those non-monastic people who are working far from their own homes today, I cannot say. Perhaps some will discover times and special places when and where they will be able both to read some of the Word of God and then to let that Word which they have pondered grow into a useful prayer. Indeed for some the use of tapes and walkmans may become a possibility. But what the person who is seeking God cannot afford to do is to presume that there is absolutely nothing he or she can do to integrate these fundamental elements of *lectio* and *prayer* into the context of their ordinary lives.

Here, however, let us focus on the work we actually do and on some words of very practical advice which we find in the Rule and which without a doubt are worthy of acceptance. I will mention only three and leave it to the reader to apply them to whatever situation he or she is in. The first two 'words' concern relationships with other people and the third is wise advice about the making of decisions.

1) The monk who was responsible for the property of the monastery and for the storing and the distribution of what was required, was called the Cellerar. In fact, though subject to the Abbot, he had charge of everything.[1] What is not difficult to imagine, therefore, is that in a large community this could quite often be a difficult and a demanding task. Indeed our own experience of stress-filled jobs may make it very easy for us to imagine that at times he might get irritable with a person who was looking for what was in fact no longer there or looking for it at an inconvenient hour. So when we read that Benedict advised 'above all things let him possess humility and, if he has not any other thing to give, let him provide a good word in reply,'[2] we can have quite a good idea of what the Cellerar at times may actually have said! I

am in fact reminded here of that encouraging verse of Paul about the value and the use of words. It was 'let only talk that is good and edifying come out from your mouths.'[3] That goal of edifying, or of building up the brethren, was most important to the mind and heart of Benedict but when he spoke of stressful moments he preferred to quote for us a sentence from the Book of Sirach, or Ecclesiasticus: 'a good word is above the greatest gift.'[4] That is indeed a pithy phrase and one which may be well worth while remembering.

2) The second 'word' concerns attention to the needs of those who may be overworked. As overseer, this was always a preoccupation for the author of the Rule. As his own monastery began to grow there was of course much to be done and certainly he wanted everything done well. This was declared explicitly in connection with the guesthouse when he wrote 'let all be done by prudent people in a prudent way.'[5] In consequence it would be strange if good, efficient management were not a major hope which he was ready to apply to every section or department of the monastery. Yet Benedict was more concerned with people and their welfare than with productivity or mere material efficiency. The goal which he proposed both for himself and for his own disciples therefore was not one of ruthless competition, but of genuine concern for one another. Or, to use a modern example, they were to become like those disabled children whom I once saw running in a sports day race. Before they reached the winning tape, one who had up till then been doing very well, tripped over something and then fell. Another, who would otherwise have won quite easily, just stopped and picked up his companion. Not what had been recommended by his trainer nor what would be recommended by the leaders of the business world today. But Benedict who wrote 'let help be given to the weak,'[6] would certainly have smiled approvingly.

3) The third 'word' which I want to underline at this point is about the making of decisions. In the Rule it is laid down that when important matters need to be considered, 'let the Abbot call the whole community and himself set forth the matter.'[7] Then it goes on to provide an explanation which to say the least is interesting: 'the reason why we say that all should be invited is that often God reveals the better course

to be pursued to those who are the younger.'[8] While at first that might appear surprising, it certainly suggests a way of thinking which is wise, as many people in the world of business are beginning more and more to recognise. It is a way of helping each and every person who is anyway concerned with what is happening to understand whatever problem has arisen and, when all has been debated and discussed, to take on board more easily whatever seems to be the best solution at the time.

However, what may be of extra interest is to note that this is but the social application of a basic principle of Benedict which may at times be even more important for the private lives of individuals. It is 'let all be done with counsel so that there may be no reason to repent.'[9] But, while that obviously can be very true, the application of the principle is no less necessary when a lot of people (or a whole community) will be affected by decisions which are to be made.

As each of the above 'words', were inspired, not only by the human wisdom of the saint, but also by some verses from the scriptures which he knew, it might be good to think a little more about how thoughts which come through daily *lectio* can influence the way we do our daily work.

According to the Rule there was in fact a lot of time allotted for the reading and the pondering of scripture and in consequence the attitude and wisdom of the sacred writers must have had a major influence on all that those first Benedictines thought and did and said. Moreover when it speaks about the Abbot and his role, it says that he himself is not to teach or to command what is against the Law of God.[10] That is of course another way of saying that he must instruct and guide his own disciples in accordance with the scriptures. That in fact was illustrated by the 'words' which we have seen above. However in this present age most minds are formed by other things, not least by what the media report, and so to hear, to read and to reflect on what the scriptures say can be not just a new experience, but one which can at times be very challenging as well. It can give us a new and fresh perspective on the short and long-term value of the work we do and, if we are to keep on doing it, it may suggest some ways in which we can improve the atmosphere and even certain structures of whatever situations we are in.

A daily meditation of the scriptures can in consequence have practical and very good effects. Exposure to prophetic people and to Christ himself will, for example, tend to humanise our attitudes to those with whom we work and so the quality of any work we do may also be improved. In this connection let me mention what I call the fact of scripture-work convergence. It can happen thus: I read a section of the scriptures in the morning and then, having pondered it awhile, go off to tend to other things. A verse which I have read, however, may remain with me or, better still, I may have chosen it as my companion for the day. Then, maybe unexpectedly, that verse may suddenly become more meaningful when I am focusing on something else or something else may be enlightened by that verse which I had read. Convergence will have taken place and life may therefore change and in the end be better for all those who are involved.

That is in fact what seems to have occurred when Benedict himself was grappling with the thought that people, even monks, are different and so do not too easily respond to an injunction to behave alike. He was about to write the chapter in his Rule about the quantity of wine which monks should drink. What should he do? His preference, it seems, was to exclude it altogether just as Paul, when writing about marriage had a preference for advocating celibacy.[11] It is therefore tempting to suppose, in view of what took place, that Benedict had read the Pauline passage in the morning and then, grappling with the question about how much wine a monk should drink, recalled that in another place Paul had declared that *each one has his proper gift from God*.[12] So while a lot of people might be more inclined to have a regimented, less humane approach to solving problems, Benedict was able, thanks in no small way to his own daily *lectio*, to face the ordinary situations of each day and then to make decisions which would be not only practical and wise, but also beneficial for the lives of all concerned.[13]

This leads me to my final thought. It is about the way that prayer, that other leg of the Benedictine stool, can help and influence our work. The Rule, as we have seen, provided certain periods of time each day for prayer and so it would have been expected that what happened then would have its influence on how the work which was assigned for other times was done. However, while most of the prayer which was envisaged in the Rule was that which was the daily celebration of the whole community, it was accepted that the words of scripture which the mind would gather at such moments could and would lead all those who were seeking God into a personal and time-unlimited relationship with him. So prayer, in its more general sense, would have become for many of the followers of Benedict as natural as breathing. Thus a short phrase or some loving words which could be frequently repeated would quite easily become for them, not just a grounding anchor, but a kind of background music to whatever work they had to do. Indeed when some task which would occupy the mind completely was to be performed, the heart accustomed to relating prayerfully to God could keep on reaching out to, or accepting, him, until the situation changed and that subconscious prayer could harness once again the energies of the mind. Thus could a certain calmness grow which could affect all those who were involved

But there are two particular points concerning prayer which should be made in any article or presentation which concerns the element of work. The first is that it should not separate the person praying from the task which he or she has to perform. If that were to occur one might suspect that there could be some elements of escapism involved. But, even though some problems can repel us just because they are annoying and apparently insoluble, that may just mean that they need to become inserted more and more into the texture of the prayer of those concerned. The second point is positive. It is that prayer should change us and expand us so that we will then be able to perceive the work we have to do and all the people in it as a part of the creative plan of God. Our prayer should consequently help us to perceive what we should really do and how to do it so that others will in turn be helped to make their contributions in a way which benefits us all.

This chapter was to have been called 'Work and the Benedictine Tradition' but if it was it would have had to treat of all the different kinds of work which Benedictine monks have undertaken down the centuries. Another title, more appropriate could have been 'Work, Inspired by *Lectio* and Prayer'. I settled in the end for 'Work – a Benedictine Insight' but because this 'insight' is concerned with many different, if related, points. It might be useful to recall the main ones here. They are:

a) the need to understand and to approach all work within a three-fold structure of the day.

b) particular advice concerning how to speak to others, then concerning those around us who are overworked or stressed and finally concerning how a wise decision can be made.

c) the way that *lectio* can help us to discern what should be done and how the principle of convergence works.

d) the way that prayer can change us so that we will have a better view of what needs to be done and how in fact it can enable us to make the contributions which we should.

But to conclude, perhaps it could be said that there is one injunction of the Rule which sums up in a very special way the mind and heart of Benedict concerning everything we do. It can be found within the chapter which refers to and instructs the craftsmen of the monastery but surely it could be applied as well to any other group or to an individual who has some job to do. I leave it to my readers to decide how it fits into all the other points that I have made. It is the simple wish that 'in all things God will be glorified'.[14]

PART TWO

Christ

> We shall rise in the brightness of the sun
> that is
> in the glory of Jesus Christ.
> We who believe in and worship the true sun,
> Christ,
> will not ever perish,
> nor will those who do his will.
> (St Patrick, *The Confession*)

Who do you say that I am?

This is, perhaps, the most important question in the Bible! Certainly there have been moments when, suggesting it to someone on retreat, I have asserted that it is. The ordinary elements of his or her own spiritual life, including those of which I have already spoken, would by then most probably have been discussed. So I could well have moved our conversation to the Jesus-question to discern if he had any special place in his or her relationship with God. Was he, for instance, only one of many people of whom he or she had heard, or did he hold a greater or indeed unique place in that person's daily life? The answer would decide a lot.

When Jesus asked this question, 'Who do you say that I am?'[1] it was to his immediate disciples, and when he was very much aware that many different things were being said about him by the people of his time. So possibly what he was thinking was that it would help both them and their relationship with him if they could clarify their probably confused ideas. If that in fact was what was in his mind he was no doubt correct and certainly there are occasions, as I have suggested, when we all could profitably do the same. Indeed there comes a time in every meaningful relationship when it is useful to examine it to see if what we think the other is is fantasy or fact, and then, if possible, to say what the relationship is really all about. When that relationship is with the one who has been called the Christ, the question is no less important. But, if we discover this to be a question which is difficult to answer, we at least could let it stay with us while on the vital level we become progressively united with that person, Christ, whom I am here presuming has become to some degree important for our lives.

'Who is he?'
As we continue in our time for *lectio* to read and ponder what the gospel stories say, what does become quite clear is that a lot of people were attracted to that man who came from Nazareth. For some it was because he seemed to have a healing power which drew them to himself. For others, like the rich young man, it was a need within themselves to have some guidance for their lives. It could however be observed that his own family, who were the ones who should have known him best, were less enthusiastic if not dubious about his much reported 'gifts' and maybe even more so of the way of life which he had chosen for himself. So we discover what we could have guessed: that different people looked at him from their own different situations and in consequence they thought of him in many different ways. That fact gives us a realistic context to his question which has echoed down the ages: 'Who do you say that I am?' However, if we want to try to find our own particular answer, we could keep in mind what other people have considered him to be, but at the same time we should note how we ourselves have been relating to him in our lives. Then we may glimpse at least some aspect of his personality and so discern how our relationship with him should grow.

For our consolation let us note that when that probing question was first put to the disciples it did not lead them to formulate an answer which was perfectly correct. They were but people of their time and so would have been influenced, in different degrees, by the desires and mind-sets of their own contemporaries. They consequently would have been expecting that, through somebody, God would restore to them the kingdom which had once been theirs and so quite easily they could have hoped, and then at times presumed, that that expected somebody was he. In fact when Peter said that Jesus was the Christ, that is Messiah – the anointed one – his chosen title could have been expressing that same hope and probably it was.[2] But Jesus, who did not intend to be the kind of person who would do what that implied to his contemporaries, responded, 'Do not mention that to anybody else.'[3] By doing so, I would suggest, there has come down a lesson for us all. It is to note that every hope within ourselves can make us see another person in relationship to it and so, by limiting ourselves to one particular hope, we may deprive ourselves of so much which the person to whom we are looking may be able to provide. Thus in the case of a relationship with Jesus, we may have to come to know ourselves much better if we are to recognise within ourselves the hope which he can satisfy and which in turn will help us to discover who he really is.

What certainly is interesting in this connection is that, far from going down that road of personal discovery, St Peter panicked when he heard the one whom he had optimistically called the Christ refer to sufferings in the future and indeed to being killed.[4] That certainly was not what he himself was hoping for when he began to follow him and since that time he certainly had not developed a desire to walk in that direction, as his own behaviour on Good Friday plainly showed. However, after Pentecost a number of the early Christians seem to have considered Jesus not as some great king-messiah, but as one who came to serve.[5] They even spoke of him as 'servant' and a text which grew in favour was the one which had described the so-called 'suffering servant' of the prophesy of Isaiah.[6] So, could it be that it was Peter who, repenting of his earlier attachment to his superficial if not selfish hopes, had been the first to recognise and then to speak of Jesus as God's servant? That is certainly a possibility. In any case those early Christians found, what all of us can find, that just as we can think of Jesus in relation to some often superficial need and thereby limit his effect on us, so too to answer the provoking question by declaring that he is God's very special 'servant' can considerably change the way that we ourselves relate to God. It can affect the way that we relate to one another too.

Here let me mention one more text which I have always found most helpful in connection with the question 'who do you say that I am'. It can be found in the letter to the Christians at Colossae. There the author, who was probably not Paul himself, proclaimed: 'in him in bodily form the divinity in all its fullness lives.'[7]

That was a statement about Jesus Christ which, while implicitly declaring that he is unique, presents him in a way which also indicates an element which is distinct from him. That element, which is divine, was thought of by the author of this letter as a life which had in some way entered into him. There are, as a result, two reasons why I have a fondness for this text.

The first is that it helps me to appreciate the personality of Jesus in the greater context of the Trinity. In other words, it does not say that he is only man (or only human). Nor does it declare that he is simply God. It indicates instead that, while he may be like each one of us in everything but sin, he also has received the fullness of a life which comes, presumably, from someone else. That seems to mean, when we compare this statement with some others in the scriptures, that it is the Spirit of the One whom he addressed as Father that he has so totally received.

The second reason why I like this presentation flows from my acceptance of the previous one. It is that since Christ is portrayed as one in whom divinity in all its fullness dwells and since he is like us in everything but sin we can at least to some extent identify with him. Does the divinity which dwelt in him not indicate a life which is being offered to us all? To use the trinitarian way of speaking once again, can we not say that we are also called to be the dwelling places, or the tabernacles, of the Spirit and as such, united more and more to Christ himself on whom that Spirit came? Moreover are we consequently not, with him, united to the totally transcendent One whom he addressed as 'Father' and then indicated that we too could do the same? My answers to both questions are affirmative.

But having said all that we have to come back to the basic truth: each person has to journey on from where that person is. Some may perceive and then accept the insights which I have recorded here. But whether that is so or not, each one who really hears that question 'Who do you say that I am?' must try to find the answer which arises from their own awareness of the way that they relate to him. What they discover will, of course, as I have said before, fall short of saying who Christ really is but on the other hand whatever they are able to articulate will be of value for their spiritual growth. So let them note it well.

However let me add one hopefully consoling point. It is that if our answer to that question will not ever totally define who Jesus is, it may help us to understand ourselves a little better than we did. The two discoveries, as I have said before, are intertwined.

> I saw him and I sought him
> and I had him and I lacked him
> and this is and should be
> our ordinary undertaking in the life,
> as I see it.
> *(Julian of Norwich)*

Christ, the Inclusive Person

An attractive utterance from the Rule of Benedict is the advice to 'prefer nothing to the love of Christ'.[1] Its context was the quest for God and so what it implied was that it is through Christ that one is able to discover God because it is especially through Christ that God reveals himself to us. But how can we define this 'Christ' so that it will do justice, not just to our faith-perceptions of who Jesus was and is, but also to what many people know about the goodness and the benefit of their own loyal friends? This is a challenge, so to offer some kind of a definition which will hold together both of these perceptions, I will use an ancient word and say that Christ implies 'the middle one',[2] that is the middle one between God and ourselves. However I will also need to turn that statement in the other way and say that every 'middle one' is somehow Christ.

Let us consider first this second formulation. Let us recognise that every person who inspires or helps us in some way can be considered as a 'middle person' or, to use a hallowed biblical expression, an 'anointed one of God', which is in fact the meaning of the title 'Christ'. For such a proposition we in fact possess a precedent. It is that, when the chosen people were returning from their exile to Jerusalem, the Hebrew word for Christ, which is Messiah, was applied to Cyrus who had made their journey possible.[3] The fact that as a Persian king he would have had quite different beliefs did not prevent those who had benefited from what he did from seeing him as one whom God had chosen and anointed for their good. So it is actually in the context of our own tradition to accept that God, or better the all-caring Father, is in some way being manifested to us through a lot of different people and at times through very unexpected ones. In consequence it is through our own positive, and Spirit-led, response to each of them, in deed or maybe just in grateful thought, that we respond to God who in the first place sends them in our way.

Since I have quoted from the Rule of Benedict and since the object of our focus now includes all those anointed ones who mediate to us some of the goodness which comes from the One who is all-good, there is one question which deserves consideration here. It is connected with that person, Jesus. 'Did those early readers of the Rule have what we would today consider as a personal relationship with him?'

The answer seems to be that in some way they did. They certainly were urged by many statements in the Rule to be open to his presence in their midst but that seems to have meant perceiving and accepting him in members of their own community or in those many other people who would come to visit them. But on the other hand if we go back and read the Prologue to the Rule we will discover there that he is spoken of in terms which are more personalised. He is 'the true king under whom we serve'.[4] He is the person who gives meaning to the sufferings that we must with 'the greatest patience' undergo.[5] So it is likely that, at least at times, they would have offered their own prayers to him. In fact, it should be said that, if they did, they would have only been continuing a custom which was well established. It had started in the very early days of Christianity and had, in opposition to the Arians who had declared that Christ was not divine, developed in the years with led up to the birth of Benedict.[6] So, when the latter wrote his Rule and spoke about 'preferring nothing to the love of Christ' it looks as if he may have just presumed that there would be some kind of close relationship between his followers and Jesus. He, in that case, would have been not just a presence in so many people, but a 'middle person' in himself to whom those early monks and everybody else could turn.

However let us also note, at least in passing, that today we have become accustomed to a form of prayer which is more individualistic and emotional in tone than would have been the case with any which would have been said or sung in Benedict's community. In his day it would seem, from studying the Rule, that the emphasis was on the reading of the scriptures and the singing of the psalms. So it is likely that it was the thoughts and even words which those in his community would have absorbed on such occasions that would then have moulded their own way of thinking and, when they desired to pray, have given them the forms of speech which they could consequently use. Yet that does not mean that there would not have been many

CHRIST, THE INCLUSIVE PERSON

verses in the psalter which would not have been considered as referring in some way to Christ. There were, and sometimes psalms or verses were in fact addressed, not to the Father, but to him. Yet in the last analysis Christ would have still remained for all of them the central and climatic person through whom they were able to approach the One who is the Father of us all.

Let us return, however, to the thought that everyone can be a 'middle-person' and consider how that insight helps us to appreciate the people whom we meet each day. I am not saying that such people are not also ordinary human beings who in different ways relate to one another in this complicated world. They are, and if that seems to be a merely secular approach, it is not just a valid but indeed a very necessary one. However, what is worthwhile noting is that even such a secular approach does not exclude the possibility of anyone perceiving anybody else within a context which is bigger, even infinite. Indeed those who enjoy that wider, deeper vision would, I hope, agree that it allows them to discover in the people whom they meet a goodness and a 'godness' which might otherwise be overlooked. It, therefore, helps them to be open to the blessings which the Father wishes, through those very people, to provide for each of them.

In all of this we can discern a mental boundary which is often very useful. On the one side it allows us to respect all those who live their lives within the confines of a very secular existence, and perhaps without ambition to discover any final meaning for what they are doing every day. With them we can and will in many different ways relate. However, on the other side of the divide, we will be able to appreciate the grace which opens up for us the vision of the greater world that offers us at least the outline of a satisfying answer to the mystery of life. Although we may not find it possible to put this vision into words which will sufficiently explain it to the people who are living only on what seems to us to be the more restricted side, to see more widely and more deeply is itself a wonderful and life-enhancing grace. For that we can give thanks, especially because to have that greater vision can allow us to be conscious that we have been called to be some of those 'middle people' through whom blessings can be given to another.

Yet let us reflect that those who want to let themselves develop in the context of this greater vision will most probably have to make an effort if they want to overcome the selfish instincts which are always somewhere in ourselves. But what is fortunate is that this reaching out to others often happens without many people being even conscious that they are denying something in themselves. The goodwill which is helping them to do all that they can has obviously grown to be a normal part of their own daily lives. In fact, I have known situations in which people have been even taken by surprise when others have declared that they had been extremely moved and even challenged by the new experience of meeting, or of simply being with them for a while. It is of course encouraging for all of us to know that just by doing what we do, or by being what we are, we have become effective 'middle people' in respect to others. But, like Paul, we have no cause to boast.[7] What we have done apparently so well has been the consequence of what we have ourselves received. In other words, the Spirit which the Father sends has mingled with our own and, even if we have to overcome some measure of reluctance in ourselves, it can and will enable us to want, and then to do or say, whatever may be later recognised with gratitude as helpful or inspiring.

But let us reflect a little more upon the effort which at times is inescapable and ask 'To what extent are we prepared to share the goodness which we have ourselves received?'

It may be relatively easy to reach out to others when our own concern is only with those people whom we recognise as being part of the society which is accepting us. But what about the stranger who is obviously different and whom we know we do not understand? Such people are the 'enemy', which is in fact the word for 'stranger' in a lot of languages, and it has always been more difficult for people to reach out to strangers and to enemies because by doing so they know that their own lives will be uncomfortably changed. However, since from time to time we almost certainly will be confronted with this kind of challenge, we can only do as Benedict advised and gird our loins with faith and then walk with the gospel as our guide.[8] Then, for example, we will hear of the Samaritan who was not liked yet who with unexpected goodness could reach out to one whose people had rejected his.[9] That both can and should remind us of the people whom we have, in our own lives, found difficult but who may have a goodness which, if found, would change our attitude to them. In consequence, the gospel word may offer us the grace we need to do what should be done. Indeed when all the hesitations which can hinder us are overcome, we may, with unexpected joy, discover that we have in fact helped somebody to realise what up till then had seemed impossible, that even he, or she, belongs to God's own spiritual family.

So we are only 'middle people'! That at first, perhaps, may not sound such a stimulating term. Yet we are called to be no less than what the greatest 'middle-person' was, that is one who had come to do the Father's will and who, despite the cost, would do it so transparently that those who saw him would perceive the Father too. However, let us not forget that he, who so revealed the Father, could and did rejoice when he discovered that so many had received the life of goodness and of 'godness' which he had allowed to flow through everything he said and did. Indeed, if we are to accept the total implication of the verb which in the gospel has been used to indicate his very special joy, we would proclaim that he, the archetypal 'middle-person', even danced.[10] Then at the final feast, when everyone will be rejoicing in the life which comes to them through everybody, not excluding us, they too, and we, will surely do the same.

> In one of his sermons on Trinity Sunday
> Newman warned his congregation that
> to abandon belief in God as Three
> in favour of the Oneness of God
> would mean the God as One
> would be countered by a Manichaean dualism,
> that is God as Two
> which then would bring to birth an outright atheism:
> God as None.
> *(Essay in 'Studies', Sept 1998, p. 529)*

Do We Need a Trinity?

Many years ago, at school or maybe at some other stage, we heard about the Trinity. We heard it was three Persons in one God. We heard that they were all divine. We heard that they were equal and yet somehow different. We heard that each one was distinct from both the others but, as we were also told, inseparable. Of course we did not understand it, but it seemed to be what everyone believed, and so we just accepted it. Moreover in the years which lay ahead some other people may have added to our little store of trinitarian ideas by saying that, if God is three, there has to be relationships within the deity and, since the so-called Persons are all equal, harmony as well. But once again that may not have excited us too much. It was like hearing that some family which we had never met was happy and content.

However, Christians do assemble every year to celebrate the feast day of this Trinity. But how much do they really celebrate? They certainly acknowledge publicly their formulated faith: 'three Persons, equal in majesty, undivided in splendour yet one Lord, one God, to be adored'.[1] But once again it is unlikely that in their confessing such a mystery they will really feel involved. Indeed it would be reasonable to ask if God's own inner life is something which is even possible for any one of us to celebrate. To keep my simile, is not the very fact of having such a solemn feast like being asked to celebrate the inner life of some important family, but one which does not seem to have invited us to come to its own private party?

But, let us suppose that someone whom we do know has re-

DO WE NEED A TRINITY? 79

ceived an unexpected invitation. That would change the picture, would it not? At first that person might of course have been surprised. Then later, as the thought of going to the home of what was said to be a most distinguished family began to grow, so too no doubt would his, or her, own self-esteem and genuine excitement. We might even guess that, while the date for going to that festive gathering might still be far away, our friend would more and more be thinking of that longed-for moment and of what it would be like. However, if we stop to think about all these reactions would we not agree that they must be the consequences of not just the formal invitation which that person had received, but also of another very powerful fact? Indeed do they not seem to indicate that in some way the daily life of the invited one was even then being influenced by those from whom the invitation came? That is a most important point and one which has a special relevance for us. It means that anyone who willingly accepts an invitation from another, or from some important family, is by that very fact absorbing something of the spirit of the one, or ones, from whom the invitation came. The invitee no longer is just 'on the outside looking in' but has to some extent become already 'one of them'.

This is a truth which is well illustrated in the scriptures.

For example, let us look at one short, fascinating story which proclaims how in the desert Moses used to go out from the others to a separate tent where he would talk with God.[2] To put that into our own context we should add that he himself must have been very conscious that he had received a special and indeed an enviable invitation to that very special place. However, as if to support that thesis, we are told that when he went out to that designated tent all those who had remained behind would stand and gaze and that when they perceived a cloud descending on it they would bow with reverence because they knew that God was also truly there.[3] But let us note that, while the privileged Moses would return to all the others and recount to them what God had said, there had been in that Tent of Meeting what we could consider as a kind of trinity. First there was Moses. Then there was the unseen God who spoke to him and finally there was the Spirit that was symbolised, as it so often is in scripture, by a cloud.

But this symbolic story has a fascinating ending which is also worthwhile noting here.

It mentions two particular people who had stayed within the camp and it recounts, not just that they were also overshadowed by that same transforming cloud, but also that the people all around them were amazed. Indeed, it seems that many of those people were upset (perhaps they were just envious!) and some of them in fact complained that ordinary people should not do, as those two had begun to do, what was considered the prerogative of those who had been delegated as official leaders of the rest. How terrible! But God bestows his Spirit where he wills and in this instance those two people with the fascinating names of Eldad and of Medad were his unexpected choice.[4] Indeed, and this should certainly be noted here, since they were not part of the desert hierarchy, they appear to us, as they did at the time to Moses, as a hopeful sign of what we all can be. But for the moment let us simply note again that in this short, prophetic ending we can find a similar if more extended trinity: two people now, the Spirit which enveloped them and God who, while not visible, is indicated as desiring to send down that Spirit on us all.

But can we say that such a trinity, which has as one component one or some of us, has anything to do with the eternal Trinity which is acknowledged when as Christians we assemble for its feastday every year? Moreover, even if we say it has, how much can we then say about the inner life of the divinity from which our invitations come? Those are the kinds of questions which we must to some extent consider here. However, let us first consider one more instance of the kind of trinity which we have been examining. In this case it will be that which is manifested through the gospel story of that new and greater Moses, Jesus, who was later to become known as the Christ.

He was, the scriptures tell us, raised up by the Father to a greater and better world. However, even when he was on earth, the Spirit that the Father sent had animated him. So to retain our similie could we not, therefore, say that he was conscious even then of being called to share in God's exhilarating and eternal life? Thus once again we find a trinity at work: the man who had grown up in Nazareth, the Spirit and the One who told him that he was his own Beloved Son. But let us note that Jesus was perceived by those who followed him to be 'the Christ', that is the one who in the presence of the Father would both represent and in some way include them all. So what can we conclude from that, except that they were sure that, with and in him, they would also be received and welcomed by the One whom they acknowledged to be their own Father too.

But once again we have to ask, what can be said about the always hidden aspect of the Trinity which on its feastday is at least proclaimed?

However, like so many theologians down the ages we can only speculate. For instance, we can think about the Spirit which can mingle so effectively with ours and then begin to wonder what distinction there may be between that Spirit and the One from whom it comes. We can at other times recall that verse of scripture which speaks of the Word becoming flesh[5] and wonder where and how that Word could have existed up till then. Indeed we could then even try to understand how Word and Spirit are related to each other and how they, being different, can in different ways relate to the One from whom they come. But while such speculations may be interesting and even hint at marvels still in store for us, our thoughts, however sharp, will always fall far short of reality and words will do so even more. What is more urgent for us, therefore, is to let our own lives flow and, as that happens, to perceive that even now we are in many ways being influenced by both the Spirit and the Word of God. Then we may come to see that we are being formed as Jesus was and that, in consequence, we too are able to move forward to our own fulfilment in that never fully understood life of the Trinity which is inviting us.

Is there not something marvellous in that? To be alone, as much of modern culture forces us to be, can be itself a sad if not depressing state. To be with others, on the other hand, can be for us supportive and, if some relationships develop into true and lasting friendships, those who are within them will be all the more empowered to grow. But to become a willing part of the outgoing, yet absorbing, Trinity is to receive a life which is unlimited and will not ever end.

However, are we not in some way being over-optimistic? There are certainly a lot of people, and at times we are among them, who will think of somebody and say that such and such a person does not seem to have accepted his or her own invitation to the life of total happiness! Indeed some people may go further and declare that God himself had not invited them! But what, I ask, about the complementary and more penetrating question: how can God be infinitely happy if there are some people whom he loves who will not be among those present at the banquet which he has so lovingly prepared? To questions such as these there can be no completely satisfying answers here but we have surely to admit that the all-powerful Spirit of the loving Father can do more than we are able to imagine now. Which one of us can, therefore, say of anyone that he or she will not be somehow brought into the mystery of that all-inclusive person, Christ, and so eventually come to be accepted by the One who always totally accepts his own?

So to the question 'do we need a Trinity?' we can answer that it is already the reality in which we live. What is required is that we both acknowledge that and also let it change us as it will. Then we will have a more encouraging idea of what the future holds and the security of knowing that someday we will be in that Triune Company which by its very nature will forever draw us more and more into the happiness which it forever shares.

Indeed as we now look around the universe can we not even say that there is nothing in creation which is not already, and which will not be progressively, a part of that inviting and yet unifying Trinity? What is there which the Spirit cannot touch and which will not be, as a consequence, involved in the expanding Christ and so united by the life-infusing Father to himself? In other words, let us be mystical: the Trinity, or maybe we should say Tri-unity, is really all that is.

> Our initial withdrawal from wrong is a transition
> from darkness to light.
> Next comes a closer awareness of hidden things
> and by this the soul is guided
> to the world of the invisible.
> And this awareness is a kind of cloud
> which slowly guides and accustoms the soul
> to look towards that which is hidden.
> Next the soul makes progress as she leaves below
> all that human nature can attain.
> She enters the secret chamber of divine knowledge
> and is cut off on all sides by divine darkness.
> Now the only thing left for her
> is the contemplation of the invisible
> and the incomprehensible.
> (St Gregory of Nyssa)

Is God a Father or a Mother – or just Nothing?

Some years ago I gave a course on 'Spirituality' to adult students at an Irish University. It covered many different themes and in so doing touched on the historical situations which had both facilitated and encouraged their development. At one stage in the course, however, I would make the statement which is now included in the title of this chapter, 'God is nothing'! The reactions were of many kinds, surprise or disbelief or simply one of waiting for the explanation which I was prepared to give.

At first I would just add 'well, isn't it just great that God is nothing'? Then I would repeat that statement with perhaps a clarifying note. For instance, I might say that isn't it just great that God is nothing, or *no thing*. In other words he is not just another item on a supermarket shelf. He is not even what the pronoun 'he' implies and so does not in any way restrict our growth by being anything definable and therefore limiting. Instead the true God opens up for us the opportunity to grow into what we are born to be. The God who is not any-thing is, by that very reason, liberating and potentially fulfilling.

However, down the ages people have produced, or have inherited, some mental pictures or some concepts of this totally transcendent God. That was inevitable and no doubt it influenced in many ways the way they lived their lives. We will consider some of these a little later on. But for the moment let me focus on a text in scripture which confirms that God is more than anything that words or thoughts are able to express. It is the one that speaks of and describes a strange experience which Jacob had when on his journey to his home.[1] It was of someone who appeared and, having wrestled with him until dawn, gave him a blessing but declined to tell him who he was. This story is not just an old one, it is archetypal too and the assailant in it is an image of the One we cannot ever see but who will do all that he can to capture our attention and to carry us into his own eternal life. However, if that is what he desires to do, we have to recognise and to accept that we will never know completely who he is. So, while our images and concepts of the Deity can often be of use, we in the end have to respect their limitations and allow ourselves to be assailed and captivated by the One who is beyond all limitations and all names.

A name for God, however true, is therefore no more than a metaphor. To speak of God as shepherd is to say that he is one who leads us on our way to pastures new. To speak of God as king is to suggest that he is able to protect his people and to rule them so that they will be both prosperous and free. We could go on and speak of other names that have been used for God including ones like 'light' and 'stronghold' which are often mentioned in the psalms. Such names for us are often necessary, for without them we might flounder in the rarefied relationship which going beyond every name implies. So maybe, if each one of us were to compose a litany of titles which we like, we too would find that each of them could help us when we pray. That is an exercise which anyone can undertake. But, for a moment let us focus our attention on the name or title which has had a very special place since Christian times began and which is able to suggest so much. It is that of the Father, or the Abba which was the more intimate and trusting term.

As used by Jesus, 'Abba' must have sounded either scandalous or delightfully refreshing to the people of his time. Which would have happened would have been determined by the attitude of those who had been listening. All would certainly have grown up in a world in which God had been thought of as all-holy, that is wholly other. Many of them would in fact have been aware that those who read the scriptures in the synagogue would not so much as say the 'Yahweh' name when they had come across it in the text. In consequence such people could have easily presumed that he was unapproachable and some would have been more or less content with that. But there were other people who were obviously very happy to be told that on the contrary God was so approachable that they should have no fear but could address him with the confidence and the simplicity of a child.

There are, as we can see, two different directions in the movements which I am suggesting here. The first, which comes from our desire to have a God who is approachable, ignores the over-emphasis of others on transcendence and can willingly accept the use of Abba as a title of address. The second comes from the desire to free ourselves from the oppression of too much familiarity and it can help to make us conscious that God is much more than any name is able to imply. Thus, while at times we too will dare to say 'our Father' with great confidence, as Jesus said we could, there will be other moments when our need will be to recognise the truth which is contained in other parts of scripture: that our Abba-God is totally transcendent and that it is right and good that we should bow down with great reverence and adore.

As we reflect on these two tendencies let us give some attention to another metaphor which those who want a deity which is approachable may be inclined to use today. It is that of the mother. This is interesting and it is good but it presents us with some issues which deserve to be addressed. For instance, how can we relate this kind of prayer to other forms which are in use and have been for a long, long time?

In trying to reply I will begin by saying that this tendency appears to have developed from the fact that in the not too distant past, the Abba image of the gospels had become that of a Father who was domineering and could only be approached with no small element of fear. Then in more recent decades the desire for spiritual growth led, not just to a new appreciation of what was, as we have seen, the basic Jesus-concept of a loving Abba, but to thinking about God as One who is a mother too. Thus was another metaphor discovered but we now know that it was not altogether new. Indeed two thousand and five hundred years ago the followers of Isaiah thought of God, not only as a powerful and majestic king, but also as a mother who could not forget her child.² However if we find that we are drawn to this maternal metaphor it would be good to note that it has also certain limitations. For example, just as 'Father' may evoke for some the memory of one who had not been as life-providing as he should have been, so too can 'Mother' stir up memories which do not indicate the kind of Deity that we at times desire. So, while to pray to God as Mother may be helpful, what we always have to keep in mind is that the true God is much more than any metaphor, including that of mother, can suggest. God is transcendent and completely free.

In practice it would seem, however, that most people like to have some metaphor when thinking about God. But as they move into the Christian current of devotion they may sense that every metaphor, however good, has to discover its own place within the rich and deep tradition which they have themselves inherited. Thus, for example, those who like to pray to God as to a mother may begin to wonder how their prayer relates to that of those who see him as a father. Are they, one could ask, in conflict or are motherhood and fatherhood just complementary ways of thinking about God or could it even be that one of them can be considered as inclusive of the other? While there may be people with opinions which in some ways may be different to mine, I will suggest an answer which is not without the backing of the scriptures. It is that the mother-metaphor may certainly provide the person praying with a clearer glimpse of the concern and love of God but that those qualities are not excluded by the biblical idea of fatherhood. Indeed the Abba to whom Jesus prayed, and who had certainly a hallowed name, was recognised in many gospel verses, not just as approachable, but also as concerned for all his children as a human mother would be for her own.³ The meaning of the mother-metaphor for God can therefore be considered as contained within the more familiar father one.

As we move even more into the Christian current, we will come to recognise another need. It is to let this mother-metaphor discover, not just its relationship to the paternal one, but also its own place within the context of the trinitarian reality. So, if it is accepted as a verbal illustration of some qualities which are within the Abba, as I have suggested, we must also wonder and inquire about the way it is related to the other Persons of the Trinity. Is it, in other words, a metaphor which is appropriate for only one of them or is it one which indicates some qualities which are in fact associated with all three, although of course in somewhat different ways? That is the question which needs some investigating here.

First let me say that its enfolding and disposing qualities will frequently suggest that mothering can be associated with the Spirit in a very special way.[4] But, if we consequently feel that that is where it ought to be, we should take note that Julian of Norwich, to give one example, liked to link it to the second Person of the Trinity, that is to Christ. Why? Because he is the one who feeds us with himself and who will tenderly receive us back when we, like careless children, have in some way misbehaved.[5] So there does not appear to be a reason why the metaphor of motherhood should be connected only with one Person of the Trinity. Indeed each one in its own way is often seen to have some qualities that can be suitably expressed by it and so we can accept it as expressing something which, although in different ways, is manifested in all three.

This means, to underline a practical conclusion, that when all the Christians of a place assemble for their formal liturgies there is no fundamental reason for not following the long tradition of the Church.[6] But, on the other hand, if we are to continue praying *to* the Father *through* the Son and *in* the Holy Spirit we should pay particular attention to the other words or phrases which are used. I have in mind especially the adjectival and adverbial parts which can and often are included in our prayers. Is it not most important that at least a good percentage of those parts should indicate those warm maternal qualities which we so need to find in our relationship with God? Indeed I would submit, that it is by those words and phrases that those very qualities can be most usefully expressed.

However, as we move and pray within the current which contains such trinitarian dimensions, we from time to time will be reminded of the complementary truth that God, while always trinitarian, is far beyond the meaning of all metaphors and so beyond what any human word or thought is able to convey. We noted that when speaking about Jacob, and we also note it when we read in chapter six of the first letter of St Paul to Timothy that the eternal Deity abides in light which is itself so bright[7] that it appears as inaccessible. So every metaphor, including those of mother and of father, will begin to fade as we begin to think of

God as One who simply was and is and will forever be. Indeed, let me at this stage add again the obvious. It is that God is neither 'he' nor 'she', nor 'him' nor 'her,' despite our tendencies to use such 'supermarket' words. As I have said, God is no-thing and so the best that we can often do, however awkwardly, is to accept and use at times, when speaking of the One who is divine, not just a neutral, but what I perceive to be a totally transcendent 'it'.

However, having said all that, we can relax because we have the consolation of a most important and involving fact. It is that, as the Spirit of the One who is beyond all things has hovered over and enlivened us, we are ourselves empowered to move towards what otherwise would certainly be unapproachable. Moreover since the second Person has assumed our human nature, we can rest assured that we, because of that, are totally accepted by the One who lives in everlasting light. What does that mean? It means that we who are but human beings are invited to participate – today and every day – in its internal and, if always indefinable, exhilarating life.

Love is spelt L.O.V.E.
and means
to Leave Off Various Evil.
(A quote from Africa)

'The Love of God' – What does that mean?

Not long ago when listening to a lecture, which itself was very good, I heard the speaker make some reference to 'the infinite love of God'. That thought came suddenly and took me by surprise. It came without a link to any ordinary life experience and so my mind did not catch up with his but stopped and wandered off instead. Of course I recognised the phrase 'the love of God' as a traditional expression. Yet I felt like someone on a river bank who for a moment heard a sound which seemed to come from the other side but, not possessing at that moment any way of crossing over, stayed pre-occupied with notions closer by.

What I am saying is that it is only from our own experiences of a human love that we can glimpse the one which is divine. Such are our normal starting points. Indeed to take a very negative example, if a person has had absolutely no experience of love in his or her own life, the word will not mean anything at all. How could it? Such a person would be like that figure on the river bank who has no way of understanding, much less of appreciating, what is happening on the other side. But on the other hand, if one has had some taste of human love the memory of that experience can lead that person to desire to taste it once again. The speaker of the lecture to which I was listening was to say much more about the love of God but never to suggest how he had come to understand it or to mention any human situation which could have allowed us to approach what he had in his mind.

Let us consider, therefore, those particular human situations which can help us to perceive what is in fact the source from which they ultimately come.

By speaking of the person who has never had a real experience of love I have, in fact, implied one type of situation, that in which a person is, or is not, the recipient of another person's love. At this stage I will mention only two things about this. The first is that the one who knows that he or she is loved may also know that that love comes, not only from some human person, but from God as well. The second is that, while the person who is loved may find it easier to love another, if receiving love from someone else had been his own, or her own, first experience in life it will be even easier to share that love with everyone. This is important and we will come back to it again.

But first let us consider here a second type of situation which can offer us a glimpse of God. It is the one in which we are ourselves the people who are reaching out to others in some way. Thus, for example, when and as I try to help some person I may suddenly become aware that through what I am doing God is also somehow active and desiring to do something for that person too. That is, perhaps, an unexpected thought but it is certainly demanding as it urges us to purify our own intentions (and perhaps our actions) lest some selfishness in us should hinder those whom we desire to help from benefiting from the love which God alone can give. It consequently may suggest that we do something more for somebody than we had planned to do and sometimes it can tell us to do less. In either way, according to the circumstances, we are called to total honesty so that God will be able to work through us for the benefit of whosoever comes into our lives.

This awareness of what happens in and through ourselves as we relate to others is important and I want to say a little more about it here.

Let me begin by mentioning the case of that romantic person in the scriptures who became a prophet, not just for his own time, but for ours as well. He lived in Israel and his name, which meant 'the saving Yahweh', was Hoseah. I have no idea if he had been aware of being loved by God or anybody else throughout his early life but his own love for Gomer, his unfaithful wife, was certainly remarkable. It fact it led him to perceive what up till then had been less clearly understood: that Yahweh, the all-powerful God, was also one who loved and who in fact would never cease from loving those whom he had chosen for himself in spite of their ingratitude and even infidelity.[1] The message of Hoseah, therefore, was that God desired to save his often wayward people from disaster and to fill them with his own persistent and unfailing love. But let me underline the fact that it was through his personal experience of loving someone that Hoseah

'THE LOVE OF GOD' – WHAT DOES THAT MEAN?

came to recognise the loving nature of the God whom he was called to serve.

This leads me to the following thought. It is that there are many other people in the world who must have had that same experience. I think of parents who give so much to their children, day and night. They do not stop. I think of those who have remarked that loving people who do not appreciate their efforts has at times allowed them, as it had allowed Hoseah, to appreciate the selfless generosity of God. So we can say that it is through the mystery of unfailing love for others that we too can come to know that strong and selfless love which has no breaking point at all. Indeed, if people sometimes say that they do not believe in any god, their human love for special and at times ungrateful people can, if they reflect on it, suggest a God who is indeed worthwhile acknowledging. He is the source and animator of that even totally self-giving love for somebody that they and all of us at times are able to experience within ourselves.

Now let us come back to the passive side of this experience, the one in which a person knows that he or she is loved by someone else. To focus now on this enthralling fact, instead of having done so at the start, has one quite definite advantage. It is that, with some experience of what it means to love another, we may find it easier to recognise and to appreciate the love which someone else has had for us and less inclined to take it, as it were, for granted as it often is. I cannot help but think of those ten lepers who were healed by Jesus.[2] Nine just went on their own way without a word of gratitude to him who had delivered them from their unfortunate disease. But maybe there have been occasions when we too were unresponsive to some people who had manifested in some special way God's love for us and sometimes we may have been even totally oblivious to the effort which they may have made. That that can happen in connection with those very people who are closest to us is particularly sad, apart from being most unfair to them. So, what we often need to do is just to get away and to reflect, not only on how fortunate we may have been, but also on the fact that those who have been good to us have been no less than channels, if not reservoirs,[3] of the out-flowing love of God.

But let us push this consciousness of loving and of being loved on to a further stage. I have in mind those moments when we have become united to another or to others in a third and very satisfying way. For Aelred of Riveaux,[4] that interesting twelfth-century monk, this was the final and the perfect state of love. Just doing things for other people and receiving help from them, while very necessary, were for him but stages on the way to resting in the company of those for whom or by whom all that had been previously done.

We recognise this kind of 'sabbath rest',[5] as abbot Aelred called it, when we watch admiringly a couple, or perhaps a group of friends, who have grown into one another over many years and who as a result appear to do no more than to enjoy the presence of each other. We are also able to perceive it in the gospel picture of the gathering at Emmaus where companionship leads to an understanding which the words that went before would never by themselves have caused.[6] Moreover down the centuries there have been many people who discovered it in Luke's description of the very early Christian church. Of course that new community was far from perfect, as some other sections of the Acts of the Apostles clearly testify, but the degree of sharing and of unity of heart and soul which it already had must have been quite remarkable.[7] It certainly allowed that first community to be considered as an icon of that fellowship which all of us desire and which, when contemplated, can be even for a short time, realised.

There is however one more image, if I can refer to it as that, which does deserve a special mention here. It is that of the unseen Trinity. However, as a symbol of a oneness-among-many it was not appreciated until, after many centuries of theological discussion and debate, the Father and the Son and Holy Spirit were defined as being equal though distinct in their relationships to one another. Such assertions were of course no more than intellectual conclusions, but they opened up the possibility for people to consider that the inner life of those three Persons could become a powerful symbol of the unity which always is so necessary in this complicated world. Indeed, because their life continues and will always do so, it is able to inspire us in a way which transient societies or groups, however good, can never fully do. So would it not be wonderful if we could have some manifestation of their unseen unity in every place where people come to meet, to chat or simply just to be where others are?

Our wish is granted. Iconographers have tried to illustrate the mystery of the Trinity, or should I say 'Tri-unity', and some have done so in a way which has had much appeal. Of these the Rublev icon is without a doubt the one which is best known.[8] It is of three quite elongated, therefore spiritual, figures but what is of interest is that as they sit around a table, they are doing so in such a way that there is left a place, presumably for us. Indeed although this icon, like so many which preceded it, was based on that intriguing story in the Book of Genesis which tells us that three people came to Abraham but were, or so it would appear, addressed by him as one,[9] it actually offers us a complementary and a deeper truth. It is that those who were received with hospitality are now prepared to welcome us. With that in mind we can look forward to the Day when Father, Son and Spirit will enfold us into their own liberating company. But, meanwhile, we may find that we have been empowered by them to welcome all who come to us and that in doing so, a new and living icon may be born. It is that of whatever group or small community develops from such openness and which continues to invite and to refresh all those who come to it.

But what about that question which gave rise to these successive thoughts? 'The Love of God, what does that mean?' I know I have not answered it. I have but spoken of three kinds of situation which I have myself experienced and which in their own different ways have given me a glimpse of what his unimaginable love implies. This fact that it is unimaginable is important for us now. It can remind us once again of that one truth concerning God which we can always fully comprehend. It is that anything we say or think about him, or about the Trinity, will always be inadequate. Those images and even words which I have used may point us to the peaceful yet dynamic love which is within the Trinity but they will always and inevitably fall far short of the reality.

Spirit of Life

1

To speak about the Spirit
Is not easy.

It is indefinable,
And nebulous,
And for that very reason
It is everywhere.

It is the ruach*,
The surrounding air
Which even unbeknownst to us
We constantly inhale.

It is the breath of God
Which flows into our nostrils
So that we
Who have been taken from the earth
Can live.

Yet it itself remains
Mysterious
Just like the One
From whom it comes
Each moment of each day.

2

The Spirit we receive will guide us
Into truth.

So say the scriptures
But
Since nobody can see,
Or hear,
Or smell,
Or taste,
Or touch it,
We can easily forget that it is there.

*The *Ruach* is the Hebrew word for breath and wind and spirit.

Because we cannot measure it
As people measure everything today
We can indeed presume
That it is no more than
The figment of a child's imagination.

Then
Will we not be like those
Who, bounded by
Their limited horizons,
Are no longer able to discern
That which
Pervades all things
And even flows within their very selves?

Yet all
Who let themselves be led into their inner space
Become aware
That sometimes it directs them
even more than does the spirit of an ever-present friend.

3

The bond
Which I have with the Spirit,
Is unique
Because
No other person is exactly 'me'
And so the melody which is produced
In my own life
Is mine
And unrepeatable.

But
Stirred by that same Spirit
Trees
And lakes and seas
And animals of every kind
Have their own melodies to sing,
As do the peoples of the world.
And so,
All going well,
The choral symphony of all creation

Will, by those who have the ears to hear,
be heard.

However I,
A small participant in this,
Must learn each day
To harmonise
With all that is
And then will not the Maker
of all things
Be totally enamoured
By his Spirit
As it flows
Through everything?

4

The relationship
Which we have with the Spirit
Is,
So said a teacher of theology,
Distinct
From those that we have with the Father
And with his beloved Son.

That was for me a fresh and stimulating thought
But it made sense
Because,
As I had known,
Each Person in the Trinity
Is different from the other two.

The way that we relate to God the Father
Should,
My teacher said,
Be one of confidence.
He is both loving and life-giving
And as everything has come from him
To him we can
with simple gratitude
return.

But,
I replied,
do we not need to offer silent adoration too?
A deep-down instinct told me that
The Person whom we dare to call our Father
Is beyond
All that our ever-groping minds
Are ever able to conceive.

Indeed that is the reason
Why we need the Word made flesh,
My teacher then remarked.
His incarnation makes him one of us
So that we can reflect on how he lived
And know with certainly
That,
even if God is ineffable,
we can become his own beloved ones.

That was, I recognised,
a truth both wonderful and well worth pondering.

But the relationship which we have with the Spirit
Is,
He almost whispered,
Of a very different kind.
It is
So subtle
And so intimate
That it is difficult for us
To capture it in thoughts
And harder still, if not impossible
To put it into words.

Yet,
Do not those who have that Spirit
Know
That it is in their own
And that
If they leave much behind,
It will unite them to all those,
Including Christ,
In whom it also dwells?

St John referred to that,
He said,
And so we can be well assured
That he from whom that Spirit comes
Will never cease
To calls us
And to draw us to himself.

5

The Spirit blows wherever it desires.

Just look around
And see the fields
Already white with people
Who are ready to converge.

They are a motley crew
From every tribe and temperament
Yet guided by the Spirit
They can grow into a strong community.

The gifts which each possesses
Can be used
For self-promotion and oppression
But within the unifying Spirit
Their employment will enable all to grow
Into one body
Which is nourished
By a love which never fails.

The Father,
Looking down on this,
Perceives his many children
Bound by a golden thread
And in their midst
Personifying them
His own beloved Son
Who
Knowing that it would be difficult
Had prayed that they be one.

6

The Spirit
In its first instalment
Is our guide.

It will direct us
On the way of peace
While
Changing us within
From one degree of glory to the next.

But what of those
Who have already reached their promised land?
Do they not now enjoy a rich inheritance?

What can we say
Except that they must be so Spirit-filled
That they are also somehow everywhere
Yet waiting until our own bodies
Which united us on earth
Will be no longer barriers.

Then in the Spirit
We will fully merge
And God who made us for himself
Will finally be all in all.

PART THREE

> A brother came to see a certain hermit
> and, as was leaving, said:
> 'Forgive me, Abba, for preventing you from keeping your Rule.'
> The hermit answered him:
> 'My Rule is to receive and welcome you with hospitality
> and then to let you go in peace.'
> *(From the sayings of the Desert Fathers)*

Hospitality

Is this a dying virtue in this age in which we live?

Some people say it is and even that society itself is losing something which is precious in the process. They may then go on to talk about the growing number in this western world who are so busy doing well-defined, productive jobs for others whom of course they hope will keep on needing more and more the kind of service which they give so that they will themselves have no choice but to keep on doing what they do! Moreover they may also say that, since that is the way it is, when people come together each will consequently want to know what kind of work the others do in order to relate to them appropriately. On the other hand those others, we can easily conclude, will probably feel more secure when they are able to present themselves with some kind of job-description which will let the person whom they meet perceive them in a context which, in turn, will keep their conversation in controllable and unintrusive channels. So it is unlikely that in such a situation there will be much reference to hospitality except, perhaps, as something which is marginal to the accepted purpose of their lives.

So what does hospitality itself imply? It is, traditionally, to receive with courtesy and kindness whosoever comes and, without any selfish motive, to provide refreshment and perhaps accommodation too. This is, it should be noted here, not only different from, but also more demanding than the ordinary welcome which we give so easily to special friends or even to those people who have been accepted on the basis of some interest which is similar to one of ours. Both types of people are important in our lives, of that there is no doubt, and frequently they will enjoy our hospitality as we at other times will be recipients of theirs. But here I am concerned with hospitality in both its broadest and its deepest sense, the kind which has less place in modern society but which when practised can create, I would suggest, a social atmosphere in which all other forms of interaction may become surprisingly enriched. It is the hospitality that is 'an open door' to anyone who calls.

To anyone!
The Rule of Benedict explicitly declares that when a person who is poor arrives that person should receive particular attention since the rich will always have less problem in securing it.[1] That is a statement which, because he had to make it, must have pricked the conscience of his first disciples and which in this present age should do the same to ours. Should we, in other words, not also be prepared to greet and to receive with kindness whosoever comes, not least because they too belong to our own human kind? We should, although I will admit that what that will imply for those who live in modern suburbia I am not always sure. However, let me underline the challenge which so frequently confronts us by recalling here that 'hospitality' as a word is linked to 'hostis' which in Latin is the term for 'stranger' and, to show how attitudes can slide, for 'enemy' as well! So I, no doubt, am touching nerves which can be very sensitive, but once again I will admit that I do not know how all those to whom such people come will always manage to make room for them in their own social and perhaps domestic lives. Of course most people in our western world who know that something should be done will frequently presume that there exist official groups which are prepared and qualified to cope with many of such peoples' fundamental needs. But let not that absolve us from concern. Would not the work of all those groups be made much easier if we and many others would support them by our basic attitude and, when some opportunity is found, by making our particular contribution to it too?

Does all this mean, one could ask here, that those who wish to practise hospitality in its most open form should, therefore, do so without any qualifying clause? The answer is, of course, affirmative for certainly that is what hospitality implies.

However, such a practice will not normally exclude the hope that those who are received will not abuse the generosity of those who have befriended them. Unfortunately that is not what always happens and there consequently may be consolation for some hospitable people in the story of a very wise, old desert monk. It tells us that on one occasion he, when saying farewell to a guest, gave him a message for another monk to whom that guest was going and with whom he hoped to stay. The message was itself a strange one but not easy to forget and so the guest, although a bit bewildered readily agreed. He then set out for him who could be thought of as the next one on his sponging list. But when he reached that other monk and had delivered the entrusted message which was simply that 'there is no need to water the plants' he found to his dismay that, while he was received with courtesy, the welcome suddenly became less warm than it had been.[2] The moral of the story obviously is that those who hope that gracious hospitality will be a normal and important part of their own way of life do have a right to live their lives in such a way that true and truly useful hospitality will always be a possibility.

The author of the Rule of Benedict to which I have referred so frequently would certainly have nodded in agreement. Even if he had not heard that story he already had included in his Rule a long, instructive chapter on this sometimes-problematic subject. It began by echoing the old and wonderful tradition that a guest, who may appear at any time, should be received, with not just charity, but even with enthusiasm. Yet because in this case it would be not just one person who would have to play the host, but in some way a whole community, he was predictably concerned that its own inner life would not be over-burdened or upset by those who came to visit or to stay. No doubt he had discovered that there is so far than anyone can go, especially if other people are involved. Indeed he may have even felt at times the pain of having to admit to somebody that he and his community were actually failing him or her, while at the same time hoping that some other person, or some other group, which was more suitably equipped would be able to provide the help which he discovered he could not provide. In any case he wanted his community to do some careful planning so that whosoever did arrive would be not only well received, but also treated with at least respect and courtesy.

In this connection let us note a thought-provoking word which Benedict, when speaking about welcoming a guest, employed. It is *humanitas*. This could be, and it sometimes is, translated as 'consideration' or as 'kindness' and both words have their own value. But a recent commentary speaks of it as 'fellow-feeling'[3] which seems to imply a quality of empathy which often is so needed in this present age. In any case, although it was a monastery with its own pattern of life to which the guest had come, what Benedict desired was that whatever happened was to take place in a way which totally respected and as much as possible accepted whosoever came. Let all *humanitas* be shown to him or her was his request.[4] Indeed, no blessing can avoid or by-pass the humanity of those by whom it is both given and received.

This kind of hospitality will obviously help a lot of people who desire to be accepted as they are, but here I would suggest that it is beneficial, even necessary, for the ones who offer it as well. Indeed it forces them to stop what they are doing, then to listen to another and, when they have overcome whatever blockages they may have had, to find within themselves a calm and womb-like place so that those who have come will truly feel accepted and at home. It could perhaps be truly said that women tend to operate more easily at this receptive level and can, therefore, much more readily provide a heartfelt welcome than their men-folk often can. Yet men have their own ways of welcoming and those who benefit can feel no less accepted or respected in the liberating atmosphere which they should then be able to enjoy. While I am saying nothing here about the effort which a woman often has to make in such a situation, it is probably correct to say that if a man has to provide a comparable welcome he will have to find what the psychologist will call the feminine within himself. In either case, with all the pressures in society today, we all need to discover ways to deepen our more personal potential and the way of hospitality is surely one of them.

This leads us to a precious insight that goes back at least to the evangelists and could be usefully considered now. It is that, while the one who welcomes can and should be Christ-like in accepting those who come, those who arrive are to be welcomed as if they were he, which in a sense they are. Is that not what was indicated in the gospel when it passes on the words of Jesus,

'What you did to any of my brethren, you did to me.'[5] However, this does not mean that all those who come to us are not to be received and welcomed for themselves or, putting that another way, that we receive them just because we think it pleases someone else, as I once heard an easily offended person say. That certainly would be intolerable. But, if they are perceived to be some of the 'middle people' whom God sends to us, then we can both accept and honour them for whom they are and, at the same time, be content to know that in a Christ-associated way they, too, can be the bearers of important blessings for ourselves. So while they hopefully will be in some way blessed by being in our presence, we may often find that through them we are helped in some way too.

Yet let us note that such a situation in which everyone can grow is but a sign and foretaste of a greater and more permanent reality.

Do not the gospels often speak about the after-life as if it were a banquet to which everyone may come? They do,[6] and there, presumably, we all will be accepted as most-honoured guests by the eternal God who gives us everything. But are we dealing here, the sceptic might enquire, with fantasy or fact? No doubt there is in many ways an element of fantasy in this but that does not mean that it does not illustrate a basic hope which is in fact inspired. So our own deepest instincts point us to a heavenly Jerusalem where all those who arrive will be received with courtesy. That is a thought which may encourage us to give a welcome now to everybody whom we meet, for one day in the future they may be among those who will welcome us.

The Building of Community

*A community is only a community
when the majority of its members is making the transition
from 'the community for myself' to 'myself for the community',
when each one's heart is opening
to all the others, without any exception.*
(Jean Vanier)

Far and Near

Not long ago I had a conversation with a bishop.

He was saying that today we who are living in the western world have lost the sense of solidarity which once we had. So many people have become, not only individualistic in their lives, but often very selfish too! I thought of Africa, where I had lived for many years. The sense of solidarity had been so obvious among the people there. Indeed those in the areas that I knew best were living in extended families and in the context of their tribal group. In such a situation everything was everyone's and all decisions were arrived at in the context of community. It seemed a very different world.

However, while the mutual dependence which one finds in places such as Africa can guarantee that everyone is cared for, it is also able to create a situation that can be unfortunately stifling. So, when many of the younger people move into the cities they discover that to stand on one's own feet can be a liberating and then, hopefully, a growth experience. But as their change of domicile, and subsequently of mentality, takes place the solid social bond which they had up till then enjoyed with their own family and tribe is slowly but inevitably lessened. That of course, although they would not be too conscious of it at the time, is but the first step in a process which has now developed in the western world enormously. So we today, the bishop said, are seldom more than temporally shocked when, for example, we are told about some child in India who suffers malnutrition or abuse. In fact it does not take too long before the news of such a far-off tragedy will slip quite easily from our minds, because of course we know that that child is not ours. And yet, the bishop added with some emphasis, it is. Then I was suddenly aware, and maybe more than I had been before, that what he said was true.

I do, however, like to check with scripture when I get a new idea. That is the consequence of having given so much time to *lectio*. So I attempted to recall what had been written in those sacred books that would be pertinent to this idea of a relationship with someone far away, and as I did some words of Paul came to my mind. They were from what we call his second letter to his own community at Corinth. Then, when I had read and pondered them afresh, it seemed to me that what the bishop said had definitely been supported by at least the basic attitude of Paul. He, Paul, was very much aware that certain people who were living in a distant place were in some special way united to the Christians of the church at Corinth and, as they were also suffering at the time, deserved not just their sympathy, but also some substantial help as well.

Paul's focus in that letter was of course on those to whom he wrote, so maybe we should first look at the way he tried to make them conscious of the obligations which they had to one another. They, in his eyes, were a group of people who like many in our cities of today were often struggling and competing in a lot of different ways. He consequently used what would have been a well-known metaphor to illustrate to them how much they were in fact dependent on each other too. He said, as we all know, that they were like a body which has many parts and that each one, while being different and indeed unique, had something very special which was necessary to the rest.[1] In other words he wanted to encourage in each one of them, not just a sense of individuality, which by itself can easily degenerate into a selfishness, but also the awareness of the needs of other people and a willingness to serve them in whichever way they could.

Some of those people who belonged to his communities were called apostles, which may have included people like himself who were considered to have had a special and direct commission from the Risen Lord. But, having mentioned them, he added that among the others there were those who were perceived to be prophetic, or to be accepted teachers and a number who were recognised as having some most valuable healing gift.[2] However, writing later to the church at Rome, which at the time he had not ever visited, he made a useful mention of those many ordinary 'helpers' without whom communities would not exist at all. He even made a happy reference to those who do their acts of mercy cheerfully.[3] In other words he knew that each and every person has some gift which can and should be used for others and he wanted to proclaim and emphasise that most important fact.

But what appears to me to be particularly relevant to our present subject is that Paul perceived that all the different gifts which different people used in building up relationships were no less than the different ways in which the Spirit worked through each of them. So, with Paul's own authority, we now can say that the essential bond which was uniting all who were in his communities and which can now unite all those who are in ours is, not just our humanity, much less some common interest which we have. It is the presence of that operating Spirit. Consequently it is in that Spirit and with its assistance that we too are able to discern how to relate effectively to those who are in need.

But let us come back to that child in distant India.

Remembering what Paul has said about the different gifts which we can use to help our neighbour, let us ask again 'was he aware that those in his communities were also in some way responsible for others who were living in a far-off place?' He was. He even wrote to his community at Corinth to exhort them to do something to relieve the sufferings of the Christians who were living in what certainly in those days was a distant place, Jerusalem.[4] In fact he may have written to them in that vein a second time![5] However, in the end the Christians both in Corinth and in near-by places took up a collection which was later given to their fellow-Christians who were suffering from hunger in the famine which at that time seems to have afflicted all the Middle East. That was, it should be said, a generous response and one which was not too unlike the efforts which so many people often make today to help humanitarian societies whose workers do their best in troubled lands. But let us notice certain clues which indicate that Paul himself was conscious of a deeper level of relationship in all of this than one of just a shared humanity. The first clue is that when he was referring to the members of the church at Corinth he referred to them as 'saints'.[6] The second is that when he spoke of those who would receive whatever contribution his communities would make he was prepared to use the same word, namely 'saints'.[7] In consequence we can affirm that he perceived in both the givers and the needy God's own sanctifying Spirit. So, despite the differences of place and even race, he knew it was that Spirit that was urging those in his communities to be attentive and then generous to their own fellow-Christians who, although unseen and far away, were suffering and in distress.

Of course, one may object and say that in both cases Paul was thinking only of the bond and obligations which exist between those who have been baptised. So what about that girl in India who may not be a Christian but perhaps a Hindu child or someone of another faith? I know that I and all of us have some kind of relationship with her. I know that it is based upon the human nature that we share but, even as the bishop spoke about her in our conversation, I subconsciously agreed that it is also the result of something deeper still. So once again I went back to the scriptures to discover if they would reveal at least implicitly what that more fundamental bond might be. In other words, could it be of the Spirit too?

The verse which I discovered first was not in any letter of St Paul, but in one which was written, it would seem, by somebody who had been influenced by him and by a number of his thoughts. That letter was the one which had been sent to the Colossians. It did not speak of the presence of the Spirit so that we will have to return to that. But, on the other hand, it did proclaim that all things had been made for Christ and that it is in him that all things hold together now.[8] So I can ask with confidence: does 'all things' not include that now symbolic girl who lives in India? Then if it does, would not whatever help we give her be much more than just a human kindness towards another human being? Indeed, if she and we are fundamentally, and in the eyes of God, 'in Christ' is not whatever good we do for her, or for some others like her, an expression of a very special bond indeed: that of a universal if not yet articulated Christianity?

But what about the Spirit?
What I have been indicating up to now is that the gifts which Christians use to build up their communities have been both given and ignited by the Spirit of the caring God. So let us ask is not that Spirit also active when we reach out to some person of another faith or of no faith at all? The author of the book of

Wisdom seems to have implied that it is so when saying that the Spirit 'fills the world' and also, which is very interesting, that it 'holds everything together'.[9] Consequently does it not appear that the activity of the Spirit is quite similar to that which in the Letter to Colossae is attributed to Christ? It does, so what can we conclude? It seems to be that, as the Spirit holds and fills all things including each and every one of us, we all, whoever we may be, are also, though perhaps unconsciously, in Christ or, putting that the other way, that, in the Spirit, Christ is working everyone into the all-inclusive mystery of himself.

That child in India is therefore ours. The people who are living in the Moslem world belong to our own spiritual family. The millions whom we never meet and never will in this life are in their own way touched by the Spirit which is touching us. In consequence that Spirit can progressively unite us as we reach out to each other and so bring us into the expanding life of Christ and so to the eternally accepting Father of us all.

Becoming Middle People

This is the place to say a word about the effort that we often have to make in order to help somebody in need. Of course there are occasions when an act of service comes so easily that we are not aware of being altruistic. The delight and satisfaction which we get at such a time in reaching out to someone carries us along. But there are other moments, as we know, when that is not the case. What happens then is that there often is a conflict in ourselves. One part may keep on telling us that we should do all that we can for someone who is in distress. Another part of us, however, may object and not infrequently it is the part that wins. So life in its uneven way may just continue on. Yet, as the years go by, some people may begin to realise that there is something missing from their lives and frequently the reason is that they had never learnt to serve.

To serve. It is in fact a very Christian thing. By this I mean that as we read the scriptures we will often find some reference to certain people serving others, but until we reach the gospels it is always in the context of a duty which is owed to some one who is understood and often even felt to be superior. So, for example, in our time for *lectio* we will discover many people who throughout their lives were serving some particular master or some powerful king or, indeed quite frequently, one of deities of the Middle East. But when we reach the gospels we will note a startling change. This word still re-emerges but, in doing so, it now contains a meaning which is different to anything that went before. It has been linked to one particular person who, although he was at times called 'Lord' and 'Master', did not hesitate to wash the feet of his disciples.[1] He had come, he said, 'not to be served but to serve others and to lay down his own life for them'[2] and that is what he did.

It is when we allow such images and words to sink in to our consciousness that we in turn may overcome the hesitations and at times reluctance which are often in ourselves. Then we may find that doing what 'is good for others'[3] is, despite inevitable disappointments, the unlikely and yet certain road to the contentment, if not happiness, that we desire.

St Paul, when writing to the Christians of the church at

Corinth and then later to those who were resident in Rome, enumerated different ways in which the people whom he knew were able to contribute to the welfare of each other. His own lists are interesting but more important for us at the moment is to note his underlying purpose in composing them. It was to help the different members of those churches to perceive that what they may have thought of as their special talent was in fact a 'gift' which could and should be used for others and the common good. So none, he said, should boast of being better than another nor should anyone conclude that he or she is less than anybody else. Instead they all had reason to give thanks to God from whom their own particular gift had come and then to use it generously for the benefit of those around them as the animating Spirit would suggest.

This Spirit moves through everyone although, as I have said, according to the gifts of each. So, to appreciate how all the contributions of so many different people can converge to make society a better place, it might be useful to recall the image of the orchestra of which I spoke before. Indeed to spend some quiet time considering the work which we and other people do as different melodies within a symphony may help us, not just to appreciate the efforts which so many others make each day, but also to release the harmonising power which is within our own.

Of course from time to time this exercise may also challenge us. It may suggest that what we do does not add anything of value to the lives of other people and at times it may go further and suggest that it would be much better for society as well as for ourselves if we could leave the job that we are in and find another one. But, on the other hand, when we observe that all is going even relatively well, we will be able to rejoice because we will become aware that what we do is music to the ears of somebody as well as beneficial to society as a whole. Indeed that very knowledge may encourage us to stay attentive to the indications of the expert and divine Conductor, so that in his Spirit our own contributions to all those whose lives at one time or another touch our own may be, not only done professionally well, but also executed in a way which is humane and very kind.

In this connection I recall a story which was told about Pope John XXIII. It was that one day when he was addressing his assembled cardinals he declared, 'It is not true that the Holy Spirit helps the Pope.' They were no doubt discomforted and maybe not a little shocked. But then, when he was sure of their attention, he continued: 'No, it is the Pope who helps the Holy Spirit.' That was certainly a slant that was infallible and maybe one which is especially important in this present age for all of us. Of course, as Benedict would say, 'the house of God should be served wisely by the wise'[4] and we must surely do our best to organise our lives as wisely as we can. But Benedict was also conscious that there would be moments when the unexpected will dictate what must be done. So what is of supreme importance for us all is to make sure that we will always have sufficient quiet time so that we may become more sensitive to all those unexpected movements of God's Spirit and more ready to allow it to use us.

This time for prayer is necessary and I have referred to different aspects of it in an earlier section of this book. It will of course remove us for a while from all the obligations and the pressures of each day, and that is good, but it should also offer us an opportunity to see all that is happening in our lives within a calmer and a clearer light. Indeed it should allow us to perceive the movement of God's Spirit in the circumstances of each day and then to recognise the part which it wants us to play. At times, that may indeed be to provide some special service which is recognised as being necessary for another but at other times it may be just, or should I say no less than, to allow some other person to provide what is required.

St Benedict in his Rule left us a good example of this kind of self-effacing care. He was referring at the time to those in his communities who for some reason were upset and whom he felt were much more likely to respond to someone other that the abbot of the place. 'Let him then send senpectae', he advised.[5] That is an unexpected but intriguing word. For him it meant the 'old and prudent brethren' but its origin suggests the kind of person who would, not just understand the one who needed some encouragement, but also be in tune with his own temperament and so more likely to restore his lost enthusiasm. Thus through the appropriate gifts of someone else the caring abbot would be able to serve even those whom he himself could not directly help.

But sometimes even less, or maybe more, may be required. Can we not all remember people who have helped us just by being who they were? Indeed at times they may not have been even conscious of the influence which they were having on our lives. I have in mind such people as the older members of our families or of some other social group to which we were attached. Most may have seemed to us to be the kind of people who had found the central purpose of their lives and who were therefore quite content and possibly quite wise. No doubt, they had throughout the years their struggles and their moments when they wondered if they were of any use at all. But as we celebrate their memory, which we should often do, we certainly will know that we are in their debt. Indeed the Spirit of the all-wise and all-loving God has percolated through those people in a very special way and so it is to a very large extent to them that we are what we are.

One picture among many now comes to my mind. It is that of an elderly religious sister who was sitting in a garden with a book upon her lap. No doubt, she had spend all her life in serving people in accordance with the gifts which had been hers but now she was, or so it seemed, retired. However, as I looked at the attractive photograph which had portrayed her and observed where it was situated in the booklet, which was obviously published to attract vocations, I began to feel that that was really not the case. Indeed, instead of not being able to do anything any more, it seemed that she was now at last personifying what the life of that particular congregation was about. In fact, as I flicked through the pages, I had the distinct impression that that tranquil and contented sister might be doing more for people now than she had ever done before.

Thus it is not just through all that we *do* for others, but through what we *are* for them as well that God looks down and forms his own community which will forever be, because of Christ, the perfect and belovéd image of himself.

* * *

Many years ago I read that when the early popes were celebrating Mass they used to leave the altar when the *fractio*, or 'breaking of the bread', had taken place and go back to their *cathedra* or chair so that they could receive Communion there. I was not too impressed. However, much more recently I came across an article which put that practice into a perspective which was very meaningful indeed. It simply said that it would have been inconceivable for him, that is the Pope, to take Communion for himself. It had to be received from someone else! In other words 'self-service' is not what the way of Christ is all about nor can it ever be the norm for ordinary life.

Perhaps some day these simple rituals of 'giving and receiving' will be recognised for what they are. Then they may be included in the celebration of the Eucharist in such a way that all who celebrate as priests will also have the opportunity to know how to receive and maybe, therefore, to give what they can more gracefully.

But in the meanwhile anyone who is a 'minister of the Eucharist' can reflect on his or her own experience of sacramental giving and by doing so become more conscious of those many other people who may later seek from them what God desires them to receive. Moreover, all who come to church and there receive from someone else the sacramental gifts which come from God will thereby have an opportunity to offer thanks, not just for them, but also for the many other blessings which, if they are ready, may be given to them through a lot of different people every day.

The Jig-Saw Puzzle

Little pieces
all alike
yet none are quite the same.

Little pieces
all together;
each must find its special name.

Little pieces
joined to others
but in different ways.

Little pieces
of a picture
which a Patient Hand displays.

Little pieces
play their part
in a plan which is not theirs.

Little pieces
made to struggle
for a dream their Maker shares.

> The question of immortality is so urgent,
> so immediate
> and also so ineradicable
> that we must make an effort
> to form some sort of view about it.
> But how?
> My hypothesis is that we can do so
> with the aid of hints sent to us from the unconscious,
> in dreams for example.
> *(Carl Jung)*

A Dream Unfolds

I had a dream.

I saw a lot of people, all in evening dress, and they were going up and down the stairs which circled one large, spacious and attractive room and it, I noticed, was already fairly full. Then suddenly I saw myself. I was there at the very centre, standing and quite happily holding in my hand a glass of sherry as I chatted with a lovely lady who was holding hers.

Today as I look back on that still living dream I know what a psychologist would say. It would be that I was uniting with my *anima* and at the moment was, quite obviously, integrated fairly well. But then the telephone beside my bed began to ring and in my dream my lady-friend went off to answer it, thus leaving me alone and feeling so. Of course I did eventually awake but all that day I kept on thinking of that unexpected and surprising dream. It fascinated me, although I will admit that I did not stop hoping that that lady who was with me then would in my next dream re-appear. Perhaps, though in a different way, she did!

What certainly occurred was that throughout the following years I had occasions to recall that dream and as I did I sometimes wondered what it might have shown me if the telephone beside me had not rung. Perhaps that lovely lady, who appeared to be my hostess, would have introduced me to her other guests who had assembled and to those who were still coming in. That is, at any rate, what seemed to me what should have happened next. Then, if it did, we would no doubt have greeted one another and quite probably have said where we had come from and that we were lucky to receive an invitation to be there and so a bonding would have gradually taken place. Then suddenly there would have been no longer just my hostess and myself, with other individuals around the room, but a community which she in fact was fostering by being a facilitating presence everywhere.

However, as I now review that dream again it seems that, if it had continued, I would certainly have recognised among the many people who were there some whom I had already known, including not a few who had been good and treasured friends. That would of course have made me very happy and no doubt we would have welcomed one another in a very special way. Yet as I think about it now, I am quite sure that it would not have been too long before I would have come across some others who might have surprised me by their presence in that privileged and cheerful company. Indeed I might perhaps have even wondered how they managed to get in at all. But looking back from where my life has reached, I now can see that that presumed development of my own dream would have been caused by what had come to me from what could be considered as the 'dream' of someone else. I have in mind the one in which the unexpected words were said: 'Go out into the highways and the byways and invite all whom you find.'[1] That certainly was bound to cause embarrassment to anyone who was already there. But maybe our own gracious hostess would have been in that dream too and would have solved the problem as she gracefully accepted every guest and integrated the less-wanted ones with wisdom and with tact.

But let me come back to my own dream once again because I now think that it could have moved on to express some thoughts which have, since then, developed in my mind. One would, perhaps, have been that which I have already mentioned and to some degree discussed, that every person can and should in some way serve the people whom they meet. So when a meal would have begun, as it inevitably would, each person at it would have been aware of all the others and would have been ready to provide them with whatever they required. Moreover our own hostess would most certainly have been there too and, circulating unobtrusively, she would from time to time have whispered to a nearby guest that somebody not far away appeared to be neglected and would like another glass of wine. Or maybe to some person who did not possess what he or she required she would have said politely, 'Go to a certain person over there and he will give you everything you need.' Thus would a friendly and attentive spirit have enveloped everyone so that they all, both freely and spontaneously, would have shared whatever they possessed.

But what of Jesus whom they called the Christ? Should he not be perceived among such blessed company? Of course he should. Indeed one of the gospel writers indicates, not only that he would be there, but also that an apron would be tied around his waist.[2] What does that mean? Perhaps, that he will be the one who will serve everyone throughout the meal or maybe that each one who serves whoever may be near to him or her, is he. Indeed it probably means both. In the eternal banquet the anointed middle one, which is what being Christ implies, will be both Lady Wisdom who enables us to be at home[3] and also each and every one of us, as we give of ourselves to all the others who are there.

Such is the banquet to which everyone has been invited by the One, or should I say the Three who want or wants to makes us all, and even now, into the likeness and the image of their own eternally self-giving and delight-ful selves.

Πάτερ ἡμῶν,

ὁ ἐν τοῖς οὐρανοῖς·

ἁγιασθήτω τὸ ὄνομά σου·

ἐλθέτω ἡ βασιλεία σου·

γενηθήτω τὸ θέλημά σου,

ὡς ἐν οὐρανῷ καὶ ἐπὶ τῆς γῆς·

Appendix

The following was first presented as a sermon in 1999 a year especially dedicated to the Father. Since it seems to have helped many people and because its theme is reasonably close to all that has been written in this book, I decided to include it here. Changes have been minimal.

We dare to say 'Our Father'

To speak about the Father is what I've been asked to do. However, as you know, that is not possible without referring to the other persons of the Trinity: the Son and the Holy Spirit. Indeed the gospel says that none of us can know the Father if the Son does not reveal him.[1] We must, therefore, listen to, and come to know, the Son (especially by reading scripture) if we are to glimpse through him the One whom he called Abba-Father and then told his own disciples that they too could do the same. Moreover, as St Paul was to declare, when we in turn say Abba-Father it is his own Spirit which is at that moment mingling with and helping ours.[2] So, as we think about the Father, let us do so with those extra texts in mind as well as with the memories of our own personal experiences.

One thought which certainly deserves consideration here is that, when we say Abba-Father, we are praying to the God on whom the world and all the many galaxies of stars depend. He is so infinitely great that no word can describe him or convey exactly who he is. Thus for example, Moses, who experienced his presence in a vast and empty desert and who then was moved to ask him who he was, was only told: 'I am who am.'[3] A name? Perhaps, but one which did not tell him very much. Instead it may have managed to increase his sense of wonder and of awe. Today in our society which is so full of many things, and often very cluttered too, we can so easily call God 'our Father' and, while doing so, forget how far beyond what any name can signify that Father really is.

Let us remember, therefore, moments in our own lives when we too experienced some similar sense of spiritual awe. Perhaps for many of us such a moment may have been when, like an ancient psalmist, we were gazing at the sky at night. Then we, like him, may have felt in ourselves a sense not just of awe and wonder, but of humble admiration too. 'I see the heavens, the work of your hands, the moon and the stars which you arranged,'[4] a psalmist once exclaimed. Perhaps the next time when we say: 'who art in heaven', those words of the psalmist will remind us of the 'greatness beyond measure'[5] of the One to whom we speak – and so his name which is ineffable may then be hallowed by our relatively very unimportant lives.

To speak of God as Father is to echo a tradition which has been passed down from every Christian generation to the next. But, if it is our privilege to address the God of all creation as 'Our Father' it would not be right to think that we may not consider him 'Our Mother' too. Indeed when Christ himself was speaking of God's love for those who stray he could and did compare him to a woman who is searching for a coin that was lost.[6] Moreover in a psalm, which he would certainly have known, another psalmist spoke about his own contentment in the presence of the loving God as being like that of a child at its own mother's breast.[7] Perhaps there have been moments in the lives of all of us when we have felt the same, moments when we felt secure, enfolded in a presence which there was no reason to define.

To speak of God as Father or as Mother is, however, to imply that the Transcendent One can be a vital and a homely influence in everything we do. It is for that to happen that we go on in this prayer of prayers to say: 'Thy Kingdom come.' That kingdom, which will not be any portion of the earth nor limited to any organised community, will be wherever God is reigning by his wise and ever-loving power. So, if we wish to benefit from his effective reign, which is what saying this short phrase implies, then we will also have to learn to make our own the next petition in this prayer which we are now examining. It is: 'Thy Will be done.'

To say these words sincerely may be difficult at times. However I know somebody who recently discovered that within herself she was repeating them while doing something which she certainly did not have any plan to do. The consequence, she said, was that she was enveloped in an unexpected calm which helped her to perform her task, not grudgingly or even only well, but with a loving generosity. Indeed, while doing at that moment what she knew the Father wanted her to do, she was, I would suggest, not just revealing, but experiencing a little of that overflowing kindness which is infinitely his. In changing her own plans and reaching out to one who was in need she was implicitly discovering the kind of Father that he always is.

To speak of God as Father can at times, however, make us realise that our own confidence and trust in him is often incomplete. To take the archetypal journey of his Chosen People as the valuable image that it is, we find that frequently they doubted him as they were travelling through the desert to an unseen Promised Land. But, as the scriptures tell us, every time they doubted, God provided for their needs. For instance when they thought that they would die from lack of nourishment, they found each day some unexpected but sufficient 'daily bread'. It was the famous Manna which enabled them to rally and to struggle on. No doubt if we were now to look back on the flow of our own lives we would be able to identify some moments when we too felt that the future did not hold out any hope. However, as we may have later come to realise, God even then was with us and providing for our most important needs.

Perhaps we can remember, too, occasions when he gave some kind of 'daily bread' to others who required it at the time but also that he gave it, not directly, but through efforts which a friend or neighbour was prepared to make. That is, it should be noted, how the Father generally works. We all are fellow-pilgrims on the journey through this life and so to some extent dependent on each other. Or, to change the metaphor by quoting Paul, we are within one body, 'members of each other'[8] and in consequence the instruments through which the Spirit wants to flow for the benefit of each. That means that if, in turn, we are to reach out with a Christ-like generosity to somebody in need we will have to be sensitive and open to the guidance which the loving Father gives and also to the need which we are being asked to satisfy. One fact is sure. It is that he will not refuse the Manna or the daily bread which we, or those who look to us in need, require.

Here let us note that Christ on one occasion spoke explicitly about a nourishment which is much more than ordinary bread. He said that no one lives by bread alone but by each word that comes forth from the mouth of God.[9] The early Christians were convinced of that and frequently they listened to the scripture which, according to St Paul, was written both for their instruction and for their encouragement.[10] Indeed, more recently the Fathers of the Second Vatican Council issued an important document which solemnly declared that: 'In the sacred books the Father meets his children with great love and speaks with them.' Then it continued, saying that 'the power of the word is such that it can serve the church as her support and the children of the church as strength for their souls and a pure and lasting food for everlasting life.' Today so many of us have not yet discovered, much less learnt to relish, that important and essential food. That is our loss and maybe why we often find our journey through this life so difficult. So when we pray: 'Give us this day our daily bread', let us allow our longing for that bread which is the sacred scripture to increase. We will discover there the vitamins which can improve and energise our lives.

We are progressing gradually through the prayer which Jesus gave us, but the next petition can be challenging and even slow us down a bit. It reads: 'Forgive us our trespasses, or sins, as we forgive those who trespass against us.' Certainly there is no doubt that Jesus wanted his disciples to forgive, not once or even seven times, but seventy times seven times, which means of course as often as required.[11] Moreover we are told that on the cross his own prayer was for those who had been crucifying him. It was, 'Forgive them, Father, for they know not what they do.'[12] Indeed, according to the Greek, he seems to have repeated that prayer many times. That may imply that even Jesus found it difficult on that occasion to forgive. As for ourselves, we certainly can find it hard to let go of resentment and to grow into a totally forgiving attitude. We therefore have an urgent need to do what Jesus did, that is to pray for, and to keep on praying for, those very people who annoy us or who persecute us in some way.[13]

For those who want to live, there is in fact no other choice. If we do not forgive, our lives may be destroyed, not by some outside enemy but by a growing bitterness within ourselves. But, on the other hand, when we have learnt how to reach out to people who, quite possibly, just did not know what they were doing, we may find within ourselves what we so much desire, that is a growing sense of peace. Then suddenly we may become aware that we as well have been accepted by a loving Father who is always looking out for those who have in some way strayed[14] and who is never unforgiving.

Here we reach the final two petitions of the prayer which

Jesus gave us and for many they are possibly the ones which are most difficult to understand. Why should we ask the Father 'Lead us not into temptation' when we know instinctively that he would not do that? Indeed another part of Scripture actually states that he himself tempts nobody.[15]

However, different authors speak in different ways and in the last analysis we know that nothing happens without God in some way authorising it. That must include those situations which for many people will involve temptations of some kind. Of course we could adapt the words and pray 'Do not let us fall into temptation' but, considering God's overlordship, it would not be incorrect to use the stronger formula and so to ask him: 'Do not lead us into any situation which we could find much too difficult to bear.' Indeed, we would be less than human if we did not feel at times the need to make that pleading kind of prayer. There are so many situations in which people feel so battered that they easily begin to feel that God is not a loving Father or that he is unconcerned or, maybe, that he is not there at all! When in the garden of Gethsemane and facing his impending capture and all that would follow it, it seems that even Jesus was beginning to experience the same. Should we not, therefore, be prepared to ask our heavenly Father not to let us ever be as much as even tempted to despair?

However, if we are already in a situation where we have to cope with difficulties great or small, then we can also find a special value in the last part of this prayer. It is 'Deliver us from evil.' But, while using it, let us accept that it is not so desperate as it appears. Because, to quote St Paul, we have already been delivered from the powers of darkness.[16] This petition cannot be for more than just the fullness of that fundamental gift. So we can pray to be delivered from all kinds of crippling evil with full confidence and, at the same time, look ahead to sharing fully in that life of freedom which already is the privilege of all the saints. 'Deliver us from evil', therefore, is the other side of praying for that everlasting life of unimaginable goodness which is promised to us all. It is for that abundant life which Christ, who is already risen, now eternally enjoys.

As a conclusion, let me add a word about that often added ending to this greatest of all Christian prayers.

As, with the Spirit's help, we pray with humble reverence to God who, as a Father, wants us to enjoy his liberating reign, we will become aware of just how much that kingdom which we pray for comes from him. Then, as we realise how much that Father gives us every day the good things and especially his Spirit which we need, we'll come to recognise how powerful is his re-creative love. And as we learn how to forgive and to accept each other and, in doing so, discover that we too have been forgiven, we may come to realise how much the grace of unity and friendship which we can experience on earth reflects the everlasting glory which the Father shares with his eternal Son and with Holy Spirit which is theirs.

It, consequently, is appropriate to end this prayer and even every prayer made to the Father, by confessing once again his awe-inspiring greatness:

For the Kingdom, the Power and the Glory
are his – both now and forever more.

References

INTRODUCTION
1. Benedict was born about the year 480. According to *The Dialogues*, which are attributed to Pope St Gregory the Great, he studied for a while in Rome but then withdrew to Subiaco where he lived a hermit's life. However, after some few years, a number of the local people found him and while many obviously went back to their homes, some stayed with him and soon became disciples. These he formed into a number of communities of twelve monks each. At first all seems to have gone fairly well but later, when a major problem did arise, he left that place and travelled south to another one which is associated with him ever since. It is the famous Monte Cassino. There he lived until his death about the year 545.
2. The monastic Rule of Benedict was based to a large extent on one which now is known as the Rule of the Master. However it is shorter and is recognised for both its wisdom and discretion. It eventually became well-known in many places which today are in the territories of France and Germany and was accepted as a valuable guide, not only for the many monasteries which were founded in those lands, but also for the inspiration of the laity and for a lot of civic law.

THE POWER OF THE CREATIVE WORD
1. St Augustine (354-430) wrote in his Confessions that he heard a voice which called out 'Take and read; take and read.' Wherever it had come from, it was taken by Augustine as the voice of God. 'Telling myself that this could only be a divine command to open my book of scripture and to read the first passage on which my eyes would fall. For I had heard the story of Anthony and I remembered how he had happened to go into a church while the gospel was being read and had taken it as a council addressed to himself when he heard the words: "Go home and sell all that belongs to you. Give to the poor and so the treasure you have shall be in heaven. Then come back and follow me".'
2. Anthony (251-306), according to the *Life* which was written by St Athanasius, heard the words already quoted above and, retiring to a desert place, he lived there as a hermit until dying in old age.
3. The Sunday readings in the Lectionary are on a three-year cycle. For the weekdays readings the gospel cycle is repeated every year, although the first reading is on a two-year cycle.
4. 1 Cor 2:10-12
5. *The English Letters of Abbot Marmion*, Helicon Press, Baltimore, Dublin (1962).

ENTERING THE RIVER

1. cf. Vatican Council Documents: *Dei Verbum,* 21: 'In the sacred books the Father who is in heaven comes lovingly to meet his children and talks with them. And such is the force and power of the word of God that it can serve the church as her support and vigour and the children of the church as strength for their faith, food for their souls and as a pure and lasting font of everlasting life'. This surely is one of the most attractive passages in the Documents of the Second Vatican Council.
2. cf. Acts 8:26-40
3. cf. Vatican Council Documents, *Dei Verbum,* 25 The following lines contain this useful exhortation: 'Let them remember that prayer should accompany the reading of sacred scripture so that a dialogue takes place between God and us. (As St Ambrose said) we speak to him when we pray; we listen to him when we read the divine oracles.'
4. 'I know a Great Person / of the brightness of the sun / beyond all darkness / Only by knowing him one goes beyond death / There is no other way' (Svetasvatare Upanishad 800-400 BC.)
5. In connection with a number of eastern religions which from time to time have had an influence on western religious thought, I think of Meister Eckhard (although he is sometimes hard to read) and the early chapters of the famous but anonymous *Cloud of Unknowing.*
6. Col 1:17
7. Col 1:16

THE TAPESTRY

1. Jn 8:12
2. cf. Ex 13:21-22
3. Gen 4:23-24
4. Ex 21:24; Deut 19:21; cf. Mt 5:38
5. Mt 18:21-22
6. 'My heart recoils within me, my compassion grow warm and tender ... for I am God not man, the Holy One ... I will not come in wrath.' These verses, Hos 11:8-8, are woven with the thread which later will appear in the great parable of the Father who goes out to welcome his returning, wayward son. (Lk 15:11-20)
7. cf. Lk 15:11-20
8. The so-called Deutero (or second) Isaiah preached in the 6th century BC when the Jews were about to return to Jerusalem from exile in Babylon.
9. Is 40:3, cf. Mk 1:3
10. Mt 2:13-15. cf. Hos 11:1 & Ex 4:20
11. Mt 4:2; cf. Ex 34:28
12. The 'mirror' theme was popular among some of the Western Fathers of the church. For example, Augustine wrote: 'in them (the scriptures) a person can examine himself as in a mirror and see what kind of person he is and whither he is tending'.

REFERENCES

THE VIEW FROM THE TOP
1. Lk 23:34
2. cf.Mt 22:34-40
3. Jer 31:31-34
4. cf. Jn 13:34
5. cf. Lk 3:21-22
6. cf. Heb 4:15
7. Lk 9:28-36. The feast of the Transfiguration is about the change which can take place within ourselves. The early writers of the Greek church liked to speak of divinisation as God's plan for all of us. The Western church preferred to speak of sanctifying grace because it emphasised the complementary aspect, namely that we are but creatures and so cannot be changed into what God forever is. However one should note 1 Pet 1:4 and then the prayer said during Mass when water is being poured into the wine: 'By the mystery of this water and wine may we come to share in the divinity of Christ who humbled himself to share in our humanity.'

AWARENESS
1. Wis 13:5
2. *God's Grandeur* by Gerard Manley Hopkins.
3. Wis 13:1
4. Ps 103/104. This and all following psalms are indicated by both numerations.
5. A gloss on an ancient Irish manuscript seems to mock 'those who in a hurry go to Rome / to seek the God they cannot find at home'. But maybe the author was only trying to ignore the envy in himself!
6. *The Dialogues of St Gregory*, Bk.2, chapter 1
7. ibid, chapter 2
8. *RB*, 20
9. Ps 8
10. 2 Pet 1:4
11. 2 Cor 3:18
12. *RB*, Prologue
13. Gen 1:26
14. Gen 2:7
15. Rom 8:28

LOVING WORDS
1. *The Interior Castle* 4, 3, 7
2. *RB*, 8 & 19
3. Ps 114/116
4. Ps 69/70
5. 1 Cor 16, 22; Rev 22, 20
6. Col 1:19; 2:9

AN UNDERLYING QUALITY

1. Ps 31/32
2. Ps 50/51
3. cf 2 Sam 11
4. Ps 50/51
5. Mt 26:69-74
6. Mt 16:21-23
7. Mt 16:75
8. Jn 21:15-17
9. *RB*, 49
10. ibid
11. Ps 50/51

TRINITARIAN REALITY

1. Lk 10:21
2. Mt 7:7
3. Mk 11:24
4. *Revelations of Divine Love*, chapter 31
5. *Revelations of Divine Love*, chapter 6
6. 2 Cor 3:18

WORK – A BENEDICTINE INSIGHT

1. *RB*, 31
2. ibid
3. Eph 4:29
4. *RB*, 31, cf. Ecclus 18:17
5. *RB*, 53
6. *RB*, 35
7. *RB*, 3
8. ibid
9. *RB*, 3
10. *RB*, 2
11. cf. 1 Cor 7
12. 1 Cor 7:7
13. 'Nevertheless we believe that a hemina of wine a day is sufficient for each. But those upon whom God bestows the gift of abstinence should know that they shall have a special reward.' (*Rule of Benedict*, chapter 40). How nice of Benedict not to tell us what a hemina actually meant!
14. *RB*, 57

WHO DO YOU SAY THAT I AM?

1. Mk 8:27
2. Mk 8:29
3. Mk 8:30
4. Mk 8:31-32
5. cf. Acts 3:13; 4:7-30

REFERENCES

6. Is 52:13-53:12
7. Col 2:9, cf. Col 1:19

CHRIST, THE INCLUSIVE PERSON

1. RB, 4
2. 'By the endless purpose and decision and the full accord of the Trinity, the mid-person was to be the ground and head of this fair human kind.' (Julian of Norwich, *Revelations of Divine Love*, chapter 53)
3. Is 45:1-7
4. RB, Prologue
5. ibid
6. While early Christian prayers, like those of Jesus, were addressed to the Father, a few were addressed to Jesus as the Christ. That latter practice grew when, against the Arians, it was proclaimed officially that Christ was 'God from God and light from light', in other words, divine. However, the official form, which was to pray in the Spirit through Christ to the Father, remained as the accepted norm.
7. 1 Cor 4:7
8. *RB, Prologue*
9. Lk 10:29-37
10. Lk 10:21

DO WE NEED A TRINITY?

1. From the Preface to the Mass of Trinity Sunday
2. Exod 33:7-11, cf. Num 11:24-25
3. ibid
4. Num 11:26-29
5. Jn 1:14

IS GOD A FATHER OR A MOTHER – OR JUST NOTHING?

1. Gen 32:22-29
2. Is 49:14-16
3. Lk 13:24; 15:8-10, cf. Ps 130/131
4. It is interesting that the Hebrew word for Spirit is a feminine noun. However this does mean very much when one considers that the Irish word for girl (cailín) is grammatically masculine. On the other hand the eastern fathers often spoke about the Spirit as a mother. The fourth century Gregory of Nyssa spoke of the dove as the Spirit of gentleness who gives birth to many children, which are the virtues. (cf. *The Oxford Companion to Christian Thought*, Oxford University Press 2000)
5. Julian of Norwich, *Revelations of Divine Love*, chapters 60 & 61
6. The liturgical tradition of praying to the Father through the Son and in the Holy Spirit flows from the awareness of that as the overall reality. Note, for example, Eph 2:18.
7. 1 Tim 6:16

'THE LOVE OF GOD' – WHAT DOES THAT MEAN?
1. My heart recoils within me / my compassion grow warm and tender / I will not execute my fierce anger. / For I am God not man (Hos 11:8-9) Surely one of the most remarkable and defining verses in the Bible.
2. Lk 17:11-19
3. 'The man who is wise, therefore, will see his life as more like a reservoir than a canal. The canal simultaneously pours out what it receives; the reservoir retains the water till it is filled, then discharges the overflow without loss to itself.' (St Bernard, *Commentary of the Song of Songs*, 18)
4. St Aelred (1109-1167), one of the early Cistercian monks, was Abbot of Rieveaux in the north of England. He was author of two famous books on Friendship, *The Mirror of Charity* and *Spiritual Friendship*.
5. Aelred spoke of three Sabbaths, the first occurs when we can find rest in ourselves, the second when we are able to relax with others, and the third when we discover rest with God. These Sabbaths were the times of rest which followed in each case a period in which we have to work to integrate ourselves or to serve others, even those whom we dislike.
6. Lk 24:13-32
7. Acts 2:22-47; 4:32-37
8. Iconographers do not sign their work. They were the servants of a faith-tradition. So it was only when what they produced was recognised by the Christian community as expressing its own faith that it became accepted as an icon. Andrei Rublev (c.1360-1430) was, therefore, something of an exception . We know his name. We know at least his approximate dates and we know that he became a major influence in the lives and works of others of that period.
9. Gen 18:1ff

HOSPITALITY
1. *RB*, 53
2. cf. *The Wisdom of the Desert* by Thomas Merton, No 8
3. *The Rule of Benedict with a commentary by George Holzherr, Abbot of Einsiedeln*, translated by the monks of Glenstal, Four Courts Press, 1994
4. *RB*, 53
5. Mt 25:31-40
6. Mt 22:1-14; Lk 14:16-34; Rev 7-8

FAR AND NEAR
1. cf. 1 Cor 12:12-31; Rom 12:4-5
2. cf.1 Cor 12:7-10; 1 Cor 12:28
3. cf. Rom 12:6-8
4. 2 Cor 8
5. 2 Cor 9
6. 1 Cor 1:2
7. 2 Cor 8:4

REFERENCES

8. 'In him where created all things ... All things were created through him and for him. He is before all things and in him all things hold together.' (Col 1:16-17)
9. 'Because the Spirit of the Lord has filled the world, and that which holds all things together knows what is said.' (Wis 1:7)

BECOMING MIDDLE PEOPLE

1. Jn 13:1-16
2. Mk 10:45
3. *RB*, 72
4. *RB*, 53
5. *RB*, 27

A DREAM UNFOLDS

1. Mt 22:1-10; Lk 14:16ff
2. Lk 12:37
3. cf. Prov 9:1-6; Sir 24:19-22

APPENDIX: WE DARE TO SAY 'OUR FATHER'

1. Mt. 11,27
2. Rom 8:16
3. Ex 3:14
4. Ps 8
5. Ps 144/145
6. Lk 15:8-10
7. Ps 130/131
8. Rom 12:5
9. Mk 4:4
10. Rom 15:4
11. Mt 18:22
12. Lk 23:34
13. cf. Mt 5:11-12
14. cf. Lk 15:20
15. Jas 1:13
16. Col 1:13